The Story of New York State

HISTORY

by

JEANNE MEADOR SCHWARZ

Original Sketches

by

ALBERT SWAY

Seventh Printing
1977

Copyright 1965

FRANK E. RICHARDS

Phoenix, New York

M-87438-8/78

ISBN-0-88323-098-4

TABLE OF CONTENTS

Page

TABLE OF CONTENTS (continued)

LIST OF ILLUSTRATIONS

PUBLISHER'S FOREWORD

All social studies students should be familiar with the part played in the development of this nation by the peoples who lived in the area that we now know as New York State. The lessons learned and unlearned, by those who lived here are often repeated in history.

Many educators believe that too much time is spent in teaching the student satistics such as: "How much of this or that is raised here or there and what is manufactured in this or that area?" Not enough time is devoted to *why* and *what* occurred in this area that we now know as New York State and the effect of these things in shaping the nation.

Therefore, the publisher refers you to another of his publications which should be accessible to social studies students of all ages—indeed, a copy should be in each social studies classroom. The book is the RICHARDS ATLAS OF NEW YORK STATE and its maps will answer many questions of social studies students at all levels. In the Publisher's Foreword are outlined various uses which can be made of individual maps in many fields. Also, there is a section for the elementary school student. In this section the salient features of each map are explained at fourth to fifth grade reading level. Following are three excerpts from this section:

THE UNEVEN FACE OF NEW YORK STATE

"We find the height of the land at any given place by measuring its distance upward from the level of the sea. This height above sea level is called altitude.

The LAND HEIGHTS map (map #3) uses color to show how the altitude varies throughout New York State. Beside each color in the legend are numbers which tell what the altitude is for the areas of that color.

You can see, by the dark green color, that the Long Island Coastal Plain is one of the few areas less than 200 feet above sea level.

Notice, also, the places that have the highest altitude in the Adirondacks and the Catskills. By comparing this map with map number 6, which tells the length of the growing seasons in the State, it is not hard to see why there would be very little farming done in the Adirondacks. One reason is that the growing season would be too short for farm crops.

When we study the several population maps, we can see how few people live in the high altitude areas. The INDIAN SETTLEMENT map shows that the Indians also avoided the higher altitudes. Winters were not so severe and life was generally more comfortable at lower altitudes.

Nowadays, with modern transportation, communication, and all the conveniences that go into our buildings, people live where they choose. Geography alone no longer limits the choice. Even so, we find that most of the people in New York State live in the areas of lower altitude, just as the Indians before them.

At what altitude is your home town? What other places in the State have the same altitude?"

"However, before proceeding with the study of the maps in your Atlas of New York State, get a map of the eastern United States and look closely at the Appalachian Mountain range. Only through New York State could the pioneer transport his family and possessions to develop the new land to the West.

Then, look carefully at the Land Heights map in the Atlas. By comparing this map and the map of Turnpikes and Canals with the following maps: Population map of the Indian Villages, New York State in 1790, the Manufacturing map, and the present-day population maps, you can see the connection between the geography of this state and the way in which it was settled. First the Dutch, and then the English, took advantage of the great natural harbor of New York City. Very early in our history we had founded the present city of Albany

150 miles in the interior because of the safe and easy means of transportation of the Hudson River. Eventually, through the foresight of DeWitt Clinton and others, the Erie Canal was constructed and the "Gateway to the West" was completed."

"Note that the Indians lived in these same areas and observe the reasons for this. However, because of their lack of control over their environment, they were unable to settle in large areas such as New York City and Buffalo.

Eight full pages of the Atlas show maps, color drawings, and reading matter on the Indians. Often, we hear the question asked, "Why do we spend so much time studying about the Indians?" There are at least two good reasons. One, we can ask ourselves why the Iroquois Confederacy no longer exists as a nation? What lessons can we learn from the elimination of this powerful primitive culture that could not adjust itself to more advanced white men's way of life? Two, let's carefully examine the Indians' way of living and see those elements of their way of life that could have improved the white men's culture.

You should know that the Indians' idea of the ownership of land was entirely different than that of the white men. The Indians believed that, if the land belonged to anyone, it belonged to the Creator but that certain tribes had the use of certain lands. Those tribes could sell hunting rights, for instance, but to sell the land itself, block it off, fence it, or deny anyone the use of it, was not within human capabilities. We, today, take that same attitude about water. We sell the use of it and it goes on to be used by someone else.

Possibly an easy explanation is as follows: A group of boys and girls go to a movie and take seats near each other. One of the group wants to go back in the theatre and get some candy so he asks one of his neighbors to hold "his" seat for him until he comes back. The others recognize his so called "ownership" of this seat and do hold it for a reasonable length of time. However, it is not his seat to rip from the floor and take with him when he leaves the movie, nor is it his seat for all time to come. He knows he cannot come into the movie at any time and sit in that seat or say that no one else shall sit in it.

This is not to state that the Indians were right or wrong—simply that this was their concept or idea of ownership of land. They did not understand the white men's concept until the white men became too strong and the Indians had become dependent on the white men's tools, utensils, etc. Thus, in the end, the Indians' culture gave way to that of the white men. They became dependent on the white men and soon the white men reached the point that they did not need the Indians.

The disappearance of the Iroquois Confederacy after being so powerful for so many years is a lesson that all mankind should not forget. Whether we agree or do not agree with peoples who live around us, or even those who live with us in the United States, is not the point. We must recognize that other peoples may think differently than we. But, we must learn to live in the same world with them, keeping our identity and ideals with dignity and without war. Otherwise, our society, like that of the powerful Iroquois Nation, could disappear from the face of the earth.

Nowhere in history is this lesson more clearly shown than in the study of New York State. You should pay heed here and use the information all through your entire social studies program.

Secondly, let's examine the Indians' way of life. True, they were cruel, murderous enemies in war, tortured their prisoners, and had many undesirable characteristics. However, in many other ways it was the white men who were the more barbarous and cruel to our own people. Slightly over one hundred years ago we were still chaining our insane. In 1830, over 80% of people imprisoned in the jails of New England and the Middle States were debtors, most of them owing less than $20.00. Also, during the early part of that century, women had virtually no rights at all. The services of the poor were sold to the highest bidder. In the middle of the last century, right here in New York State, the first workmen to strike for higher wages were fined and imprisoned. Until well into this century, child labor, often under brutal conditions, was commonplace. Definitely there was much that the white men of that period could have learned from the Indians. Thus, here in our study of New York State and its people, we see the necessity of examining all cultures, even those that seem inferior to ours, with the idea of improving ourselves and our way of life."

Other maps in the RICHARDS ATLAS OF NEW YORK STATE show the campaigns of the Colonial Wars and many of the important campaigns of the Revolutionary War that were fought in New York State. The details of these campaigns may not be too essential for the elementary social studies student, but the reasons why these campaigns took place here are most important. Again, we turn to the Land Heights map and Turnpikes and Canals map for the geographic answers to the question, "Why did these things take place in New York State?"

In the RICHARDS ATLAS OF NEW YORK STATE are many more maps, too many to mention here, which will enable the student to understand the reason for studying the state of New York and to apply the lessons learned here in later social studies experiences. However, one important map that needs special mention is the *Emergence of New York State*. This is really a series of four maps each showing boundary changes and disputes. The last one shows the state of New York as it is today after passing through its many stages, any one of which could and almost did result in war with neighboring states. The final boundary settlement of the state of New York, in the Treaty of Hartford in 1786, is an example of adjusting seemingly impossible problems caused by other men dead long before this period. Social studies students will be discussing treaties in many advance courses. It would be well to compare each of these treaties with the Hartford Treaty and the events that led up to the treaty.

New York State is a great state economically and historically. It is of primary importance that the student should know why it became great. This Atlas shows the student why he should study New York State and its part in shaping the nation.

FRANK E. RICHARDS

Chapter I

THE INDIANS BEFORE
THE WHITE MAN CAME

1

CHAPTER I

1. The First Indians

EXPLORERS   Do you like to find out new things? If you do, then you are an explorer. Explorers want to know things about the world. They want to know about people. Explorers are always happy when they are finding out new things they didn't know before.

Sometimes exploring is hard work. It is fun, too! This chapter of our book is going to help you do some exploring into the lives of some people who lived in New York State long, long ago.

The people who lived here long ago were called Indians. They got that name from Columbus. Columbus thought he had landed in India when he found the new world. He called the people "Indians."

WHERE THEY CAME FROM   An explorer would want to know if these "Indians" were always here. Did they come from another place? Men who learn about these things say the Indians did come from another place. That place is called Asia.

Look at the world map or the globe in your room. Find Alaska. See how close it is to Asia. Just fifty-six miles. The water which is between Asia and Alaska is called Bering Strait. In this fifty-six mile wide Strait are two pieces of land where the Indians could have stopped to rest on the way over.

The Indians could have come in small boats. They might have walked! We have reason to think that long ago there may have been land where the Bering Strait is now. The Bering Strait is only 120 feet deep. Its bottom could easily have been above the water in those long ago days when the earth was changing around so much.

WHY DID THEY LEAVE   Why did these people come from Asia? Why were they exploring into new places? The answer seems to be that they were hunting for food. That is a good reason for moving from one place to another, isn't it?

Do you suppose that they lived in that part of Asia where the great Gobi Desert is now? Once upon a time there was no desert there. It was a green, grassy land. Very large animals lived there. One of these large animals looked like the elephants we see today. However, these early elephant-like animals were much bigger and quite hairy. The Indians hunted this large, hairy elephant.

The land began to dry up and change into a desert. Many animals went away to the wonderful valleys of Alaska. The Indians followed them. This is one of the reasons given for the Indians' moving across the strait.

Indians enter Alaska hunting for food

WHEN DID THEY LEAVE   When did the Indians come? We are not quite sure. We are sure that Indians were in North America more than ten thousand years ago. People who have learned a lot about these things guess that Indians came into what is now New York State after the ice began to melt. Then the plants and animals began to come back to this part of the earth. We think that was about five thousand years ago.

Other people began to come to our country to live about 350 years ago. So you see the Indians came here a good long time before anyone else.

2. Algonkians

LIFE WITH THE ALGONKIANS   The early explorers of New York first met some Indians called Algonkians (Al-gon-kee-ans). This was a family name. Many tribes were Algonkians. Some of the tribes were the Mahicans (Ma-hee-kans), the Montaucks (Mone-tocks), and the Wappingers (Wap-pin-jers).

The Algonkians were woodland people who used the woods for getting food, making their clothing, and for building their houses. Each family lived in a house made of bark. The house was not very big. It was round, like an Eskimo's igloo.

The Algonkians were good hunters. They used the animals they killed for food and for clothing.

The Algonkians also grew things such as sunflowers, corn, beans, and other plants. That is a sign that they stayed in one place for a long time and were not always moving about. Some of the things they grew are still grown in this part of our country. The white people who came to live here learned how to grow these things from the Indians!

The Indian women put the corn seed in small hills. They put a dead fish in the hill with the seed. This would help the corn grow faster and stronger. Then they planted beans and

4

other plants in between the hills of corn so the beans could use the corn to climb on. That was good thinking.

The Indian women did all the farming work. They used tools made of animal bones, stone, and wood. Some of these early tools have been found by men who know a great deal about Indians. We can see some of these tools today when we go to the museum.

THE PEACEFUL LIFE ENDS   We know that these people lived in peace for many, many years. Early explorers found that their villages had no fences around them. This is a good sign that they were not afraid of anyone. Their peaceful life lasted for hundreds of years. The time came when they began to put up fences around their villages. People do not build such fences for fun, do they? Of course not, and the Algonkians didn't either. They put up these fences because they had to.

THE IROQUOIS WIN THE WAR WITH THE ALGONKIANS
Indians from the middle part of our state had begun to come into the eastern woodlands along the Mohawk River. These newcomers wanted to take the eastern hunting lands away from the Algonkians. The newcomers were the Indians we call the Iroquois (Ear-o-kwoy).

For about one hundred years these two groups kept fighting each other in long, bloody wars. At last the Iroquois beat the Algonkians in a great fight on the banks of the Mohawk River. This fight was at a place called Wolf's Hollow.

The Algonkians still had the Hudson Valley and Long Island in New York State, but that was all. They were never strong again. The Iroquois became the greatest and strongest Indians in the east.

3. The Iroquois Confederacy

With a little exploring we can learn why the Iroquois became so strong.

The names of the tribes we will explore are the Senecas, the Cayugas, the Onondagas, the Oneidas, and the Mohawks. Later on, in 1722, another tribe became part of the Iroquois family in New York State. That tribe, called the Tuscaroras, had been living in the South. The Tuscaroras were made to give up their land to the white men. When this happened they came North to be with their people.

First of all, who were the Iroquois? Well, Iroquois is a family name. Many tribes of Indians belonged to the Iroquois family. These tribes could understand each other because they all spoke alike.

An Algonkian wigwam

DEKANIWIDA (DEE-KAN-I-WEE-DA) AND HIAWATHA (HEE-A-WA-THA) The five Iroquois tribes belonged to a Confederacy. That meant that they would all stick together as friends and help one another. This Confederacy was started by two great chiefs, Dekaniwida (Dee-kan-i-wee-da) and Hiawatha (Hee-a-wa-tha).

THE IROQUOIS CONFEDERACY STILL LIVES Its headquarters today is at a place where an Onondaga village once stood. The Confederacy met for the first time many years ago in that village. In the Iroquois language the word Onondaga means "on the hill". Just as in the old days, the village where the Confederacy Council meets each year is on a hill just outside the city of Syracuse.

THE IROQUOIS DID NOT MAKE WAR ON ONE ANOTHER When each nation became part of the Confederacy, it had to agree not to make war on the other nations. All five of the nations agreed to do what the Council said. They also agreed to follow the rules made by the Council.

The Confederacy helped the Iroquois to grow stronger because they did not waste men and time in wars with each other.

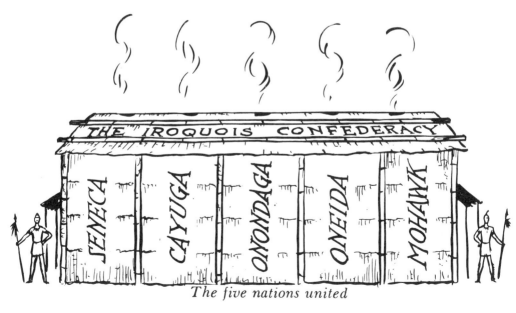

The five nations united

7

BEAR　DEER　HAWK　TURTLE　WOLF　BEAVER　SNIPE　HERON

Some clan symbols of the Iroquois

CLANS AND FAMILIES　Within each tribe there were different groups of families called clans. The Mohawks had nine clans. So did the Oneidas. The Senecas had eight clans. The Cayugas had ten clans. The Onondagas had the most. They had fourteen clans.

Each clan had a name such as Turtle, Bear, or Deer. The real head of each clan was always the oldest woman in the ruling family of each clan.

WOMEN WERE IMPORTANT　Women were very important in Iroquois life. The women of the ruling family were the ones who chose the clan's chief and the clan's war chief. The one they chose would have to be agreed to by the men's council.

A man and a woman of the same clan could not marry each other. When a man and a woman did marry, the man had to go to his wife's clan to live. If a man from the Bear clan married a woman from the Turtle clan, he would have to leave his home and go to live in his wife's home with her people. Not only that, but his children would always have their mother's name — not his. They would all be little Turtles — not little Bears!

THE LAND WAS OWNED BY ALL　The land of the Iroquois was owned by all of the tribe together. No one family owned one piece of land. It was owned by all, and all could have some of the food that was grown on the land. This was not true of the houses, though.

8

Women were important

The women of the clans owned the houses. A man went to live in the house of his wife and he could stay there as long as he and his wife were friends. If they stopped being friends, the man had to leave and go back to his mother's house to live. This is one way in which the Iroquois' way of life was different from ours.

4. How The Iroquois Lived

THE VILLAGE   An Indian village was a busy place. Everyone who belonged to the clan had a job to do. These jobs had to be done if the clan was to get along well.

The Iroquois were great hunters and fighters. They were farmers and fishermen as well. Because of this, they always built their villages near rivers or lakes. This meant that they would have enough food, for most of the time the rivers and lakes were full of fish. They would also have water for cooking and for washing.

9

FOOD, CLOTHING, AND TOOLS   The woods were always nearby for hunting. This meant there would be meat to eat. Also, the Indians would have the animal skins for clothing and for bed covers.

The bones and sinews of the animals were used to make the tools with which the Iroquois hunted, fished, and farmed. Sinews are the strong, stringlike parts of the animal's body. The sinew of the deer was the best thing of all for a good bowstring.

CLEARING THE LAND   After the place for a village had been chosen, the land was cleared. Then the houses could be built and crops could be planted.

Today it is easy to cut down a tree. All that is needed is a good saw. The trees can be cut down in a short time. The Indians, however, had to use a much slower way.

With their stone tools, the Indians cut a ring of bark from the tree. The ring of bark was cut close to the ground. Then a fire was started in a circle around the tree. The fire burned slowly. The tree grew weaker and weaker. After some time it fell to the ground. It was not a very fast way to get a tree down, but it worked.

WOMEN FARMERS   After the land had been cleared, the women went to work to grow the food for the clan. All of the farming was done by the women and girls, just as it was in the Algonkian villages. The Iroquois believed that the earth would not grow crops unless women planted and took care of the crops.

HUNTING AND FISHING   What were the men and boys doing while the women and girls were farming? Hunting and fishing, of course, and keeping enemies from their village.

Hunting and fishing were fun then, too. They were also hard work. We know that the Indians hunted with bows and arrows until the white men came and showed them how to use guns.

It was hard work to make a good bow. The Indian hunter made one that pleased him. He liked to make the bow from the wood of the red cedar tree. After he had chosen his wood carefully, he wanted to make the wood hard. He used fire to do this. Then he shaped the wood with a stone knife. When the bow was just right, it was strung with deer sinew.

Not all bows were alike. Some were light and some were heavy. They were made to fit all kinds of hunting. After all, the Indian didn't need the same kind of bow to kill a wild bird as he did to kill a deer.

PEOPLE OF THE FLINT   When the bow was finished, the Iroquois man had to make his arrows and arrowheads. Most of the arrowheads were made from stone. The Indians found that flint and chert were the kinds of stone that made the best arrowheads. The name "Mohawk" means "People of the Flint." Now we know what their arrowheads were made of!

THE SPEAR   If an Indian brave went fishing alone, the best tool to use was a spear. The Indians did not use fish hooks very often until the white man came and showed the kind he had to the Indians. Some fishermen were so good with their spears that they could catch three hundred fish in one night!

However, much fishing was done by large groups. In these groups there would be men and boys working together. Then they used large nets into which they would drive the fish. They could catch a lot of fish at one time that way. When this happened, the women and girls made fires and the fish were slowly smoked over the fire. In this way the fish could be saved for eating later on.

Eels were forked out of the water and thrown to the bank.

NOTHING WAS WASTED   Nothing was wasted in an Iroquois village. Almost every part of a fish, animal, or bird was used. If it could not be used right after the animal was killed, it was saved to be used at a later time.

NOT EVEN PLANTS WERE WASTED   Every bit of a plant was used, too. All the parts of the corn were used. The outer covering of the ear of corn was used to make rugs and mats. Sometimes, dolls were made from the outer coverings of the ears of corn.

5. Home Life of the Iroquois

THE IROQUOIS LONGHOUSE WAS DIFFERENT   The Iroquois homes were very different from those of other Indians.

Iroquois homes were made of wood and bark. They were called "longhouses." The reason for this is easy to understand — the houses were long! Most of the time they were built for more than one family. Each family had a space about twenty feet long.

The interior of a longhouse

Each longhouse was really something like a one-story apartment house without the inside walls. Sometimes the longhouses were two hundred feet long. These longhouses might have twenty families in them — ten families on each side.

BUILDING THE LONGHOUSE   Look at the pictures of the longhouses. First the men made the frame of the house with long poles. The poles were really trees without the bark.

Then the women covered the frame of the house with bark. They used bark from the red elm tree or the ash tree. When this had been done, the men put more poles into the ground on the outside. This helped to hold the bark in place.

For every twenty-foot "room" a hole was cut in the roof to let smoke get out. The smoke came from the fire that was built between the wide shelves which each family used for sitting, working and sleeping. One fire served two families.

In summer such a longhouse was nice to live in because much of the cooking was done outside. In winter it was not so nice. The smoke from the fires sometimes got very thick and heavy. Then the people living in the longhouses had to put their faces down close to the ground so they could get enough fresh air.

At each end of the longhouse there was a door. Sometimes this door was made out of bark. Other times the Iroquois used animal skins to keep out the rain and snow.

LIVING ON A SHELF You can see in the picture that inside the longhouse there were two wide shelves along each side. Each family had an upper and a lower shelf about twenty feet long. This was the family home.

On the bottom shelf the family sat, worked, and slept. On the top shelf the family put all the things it owned such as food, tools, dishes and toys. The top shelves were used as cupboards for the Iroquois family.

There were things hanging on all the poles in an Iroquois longhouse. Some of the things that were hung there were ears of dried corn, clothing, bows and arrows. One thing you would not find not find hanging there was meat. There was a reason for that.

WHERE THE MEAT WAS KEPT The Indians kept their meat by smoking it or drying it. Then they dug a hole in the ground and lined it carefully with tree bark until they were sure it would stay dry. Into this hole they put their deer meat and bear meat. Corn and beans were also stored in this hole.

WAMPUM   The long winter days in the longhouse were also used to make wampum. Wampum was very important to the Indians. Maybe you already know that Indian word—wampum. This word is an Algonkian word. It means "white strings." The Iroquois word for the same thing was "otekoa." But do you know what wampum really was? Let's do some exploring and find out what it really was.

WHAT WAMPUM WAS   Wampum was the beads the Indians made from shells like those we sometimes find on the sand. These beads were strung together in strings. Sometimes the beads were woven into belts the Iroquois made.

USES OF WAMPUM   These beads and belts were very important to the Indian people because they were used to tell important things the tribe or Confederacy did. The beads on the belts made pictures, or signs, that told what the Indian wanted to say. Wampum strings were also used as money.

Whenever an agreement was reached, a wampum belt was made to tell the story of the agreement. These agreements could be with each other, with other tribes, and later with the white men.

The Indian brave used a string of wampum when he wanted to ask a maiden to be his wife. If she took the wampum, the brave knew that he had won the maiden.

When someone died, a wampum string or belt was made so he would be remembered long after he was dead.

Wampum was used as a sign that the Indians were at war. It was also used as a sign of peace when the war was ended.

COLOR OF WAMPUM   The color of wampum was important, too. Deep purple meant that someone was dead. It was also a sign of deep sadness.

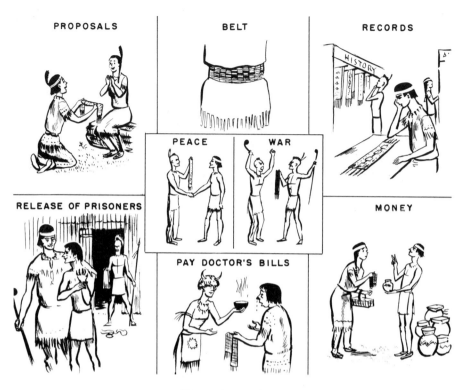

Uses of wampum

If a chief sent a belt of red wampum to the chief of another tribe, that meant WAR!

White wampum was used as a sign of peace, or of friendship.

A HAPPY PEOPLE   Sometimes, when people live as close together as the Iroquois did in the longhouse, they are not very nice to each other. But when the white people first came to New York they saw that an Indian home was always a happy one.

The people in an Indian family were always kind to each other. They could be very unkind to their enemies in time of war. However, when the war was over, they would often bring some of their enemies back home with them. These people were kept by the Indians, and they became part of the tribe.

THE IROQUOIS LOVED CHILDREN   Later, after the white man came, many white children became part of an Indian tribe in the same way. The Iroquois loved children dearly and were never, never unkind to them.

WHAT THE IROQUOIS BELIEVED   Did the Indians believe in a god? Yes, they did. They believed in one, chief god. Their god was the ruler of everything that lived.

They also believed that good people and brave warriors would live again after they died. They believed that these people would live in a better world after they died. They called this better world the Happy Hunting Grounds.

1. Why were the first people in North America called INDIANS?
2. Give two reasons why scientists believe that the Indians came from Asia.
3. How long had Indians lived in New York State before the white men came?
4. What were Indians who lived in eastern New York State called?
5. Write four sentences to tell in your own words how these first New Yorkers lived.
6. The name "Iroquois" is the family name. Six tribes of Indians belong to this family. What are their names?
7. Two great chiefs started the Iroquois Confederacy. Give their names.
8. What was the purpose of the Iroquois Confederacy?
9. Write two sentences of your own to show how important women were in Iroquois life.
10. Give three reasons why the Iroquois always built their villages by streams.
11. Give at least three ways in which animals were useful to the Iroquois.
12. Who did the farming in an Iroquois village? Why?
13. Write down one way in which the Iroquois used each of the following:

1. flint and chert	5. bear fat
2. wood of the red cedar tree	6. bird feathers
3. hickory wood	7. animal bones
4. animal skins	8. porcupine needles

17

14. What was wampum? Give at least five ways the Indians used wampum.

Write out the meaning of each of the words below. Then use each word in a sentence of your own to prove that you really understand the meaning.

1. ancestor	6. squash	11. moccasin
2. example	7. stockade	12. bait
3. language	8. fertile	13. worship
4. shelter	9. snare	14. sinew
5. igloo	10. barbed	15. porcupine

PERHAPS YOU WOULD LIKE TO ...

1. Build a model of a longhouse. Perhaps it would be a good idea to make a roof which is easy to lift off. If you do this, you can make the inside more easily. (For a good picture of a longhouse, look at the one in Richards New York State Atlas.)
2. Make some wampum. The various shapes of macaroni make very good modern wampum. The short straight pieces are easy to work with. Color them with fingernail polish or paint and glue them to a piece of cloth if you want to make a wampum belt. If you want to make wampum strings, then just string your "shells" on thin leather strings or pieces of heavy yarn. Be sure your wampum belt tells a story! If you live on Long Island, of course, or where you can find clam shells easily, you might try making the wampum just as the Indians did.
3. Take a trip to the State Museum at Albany to look at and study the wonderful dioramas of Indian life. If you can't go to Albany, write to the Museum nearest you and ask if it has an Indian exhibit. Then plan to go there on the first fine day.
4. Divide your class into groups and let each group make a small model of one of the Indian activities you have read about. You do not need REAL things, but be sure that what you make LOOKS real. Get together and decide on the size so that everything will be in the same scale.

Chapter II

THE INDIANS AFTER
THE WHITE MAN CAME

CHAPTER II

1. The First White Men

THE WHITE MEN REACH AMERICA   In 1609 two men came to North America from Europe. These two men did not know each other. They came here within a few weeks of each other, and their travels brought them within ninety miles of each other. Their names were Henry Hudson, of Holland, and Samuel de Champlain of France. Each of these men had a great deal to do with changes that took place in the lives of the Indians of New York State.

HENRY HUDSON   Henry Hudson sailed his ship, the **Half Moon,** into New York Harbor. From there he sailed up the river. Groups of Algonkian Indians came out in their canoes to see the "giant" boat.

The Indians were curious and friendly, and brought gifts of fur and food. In return, the Dutch sailors gave them gifts. This exchange of gifts started the trade between the white man and the Indians.

The Indians received such wonderful things as knives, fish hooks, needles, pots, pans, and axes. It did not take long for the red men to learn that these things made their work much easier. They wanted more and more, so they brought more and more furs to the white man. Furs were easy for the Indians to get. They were glad to hunt for the white men when there were such useful things to receive in return.

SAMUEL DE CHAMPLAIN   The Indians' meeting with Samuel de Champlain was not such a happy one. Champlain came into North America through the St. Lawrence River. He made friends with the Huron Indians who lived in that part of the country.

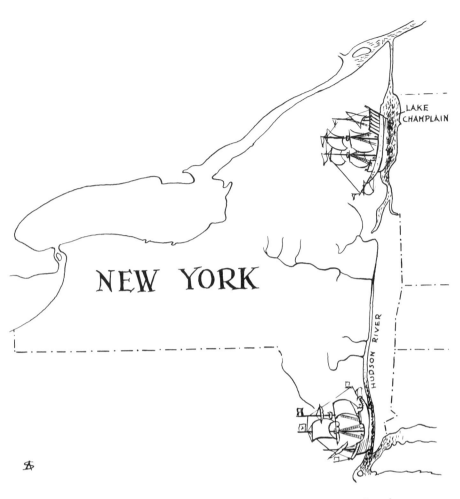

Hudson and Champlain sail within 90 miles of each other.

In 1609 Champlain went south of the St. Lawrence with a group of Hurons. He saw, for the first time, the beautiful lake that now has his name.

The Hurons and their cousins, the Iroquois, were enemies. When it was learned that there was an Iroquois camp nearby, the Hurons wanted to fight their enemy. Champlain went along with his Huron friends.

Before the Iroquois could begin to fight, Champlain stepped forward and fired his gun at them. Two Iroquois warriors fell dead!

The Iroquois had not seen a gun before. This strange "thunder pole" scared them so much that they turned and ran like frightened deer into the forest. The Hurons chased them and won the fight. That day made two things clear to the Iroquois: (1) they hated the French from that day on, and (2) they knew they must have "thunder-poles" (guns) of their own.

2. The Fur Trade Causes War

THE INDIANS BECOME GREAT TRADERS   The white man had set up trading posts along the Hudson River. It was not long before the Iroquois began trading the fur of the beaver for guns.

The Hudson River was in Algonkian land, but the Mohawks quickly beat the Algonkians in battle. Then the fur trade with the Dutch, and later with the English, was taken over by the Mohawks.

The Indians loved to trade.

From this time on, the Iroquois story is one of trade. Almost everything that happened to the Iroquois later on happened because they changed from being mainly hunters and farmers to being traders.

The Iroquois loved to trade, and the white man wanted furs. So the Iroquois traveled hundreds of miles inland for furs. They would be traded for tomahawks, axes, cloth, and knives. The Iroquois built up a great empire because they were stronger than other tribes. The Iroquois could easily win battles because they had guns, and the other tribes did not.

The Hurons, in the north, gave the Iroquois the most trouble. The Hurons, old enemies of the Iroquois, were in charge of the fur trade in the north for many years. They brought their beaver and mink skins to the French and traded the furs for metal and cloth.

When the supply of furs ran low in New York State, the Iroquois knew that they must have the northern trade, too. Many bitter battles were fought, and both sides lost many warriors.

By 1650 the Iroquois had won. They were in control of all the land east of the Mississippi as far south as Virginia. Look at the Indian Empire Map in **Richards Atlas of New York State** and you can see how much land this was. The mighty Hurons were nearly wiped out, and many other tribes were almost destroyed by the powerful Iroquois.

THE INDIANS' LIFE BEGINS TO CHANGE   During this time of trading and fighting, the Iroquois had suffered, too. Their youngest and strongest men were dead. Their villages were uncared for and shabby. They needed a time of peace.

For a long time there was peace. The Iroquois planted crops and built new villages. They traded with the Dutch, the French, and the English. Little by little, though, the life of the Iroquois began to change. The Indians' life was much easier because of the tools the white man had brought. After all, a metal axe cuts much better than a stone axe. A gun can kill more game than a bow and arrow. Squaws could sew more easily with steel needles than with bone needles. They could cook better in pots made of iron than in those made of clay. The Indians even built log cabins instead of longhouses, for the log cabins were far more comfortable and healthful, and just as easy to make.

THE MISSIONARIES   The Indians learned many things from the white men. Traders were not the only white men who came to America. Missionaries came too. These missionaries brought the Christian religion to the Indians. They also built schools. In these schools they taught the Indian children to read and write. They showed the Indians how to use the plow and how to farm. Two of the famous Jesuit missionaries who worked among the Hurons were Father Jean de Brebeuf and Father Joseph Chaumonot.

There were other well-known Jesuits. Father LeMoyne, Father Fremin, Father Pierion, and Father Bruyes were among them. The one best-remembered of all the missionaries was a Jesuit priest named Father Isaac Jogues (Zhoag).

Father Jogues was a great and good man who was treated cruelly by the Indians. We have much to thank him for. Wherever he went he looked around carefully and later wrote down what he saw. He was the man who discovered Lake George. He was the first missionary to try to teach the white man's religion to the Iroquois. His work made it easier for other missionaries later. His church made him a saint. There is a shrine to him at Auriesville, on the Mohawk River, where he was killed.

3. The Indian and the White Man's War

Between the years 1689 and 1763, England and France fought four wars with each other. Each country wanted for itself all of North America and its riches. The Indians fought in these wars, too, because the fur trade was important to them.

The Hurons and Algonkians fought on the side of the French, and the Iroquois fought on the side of the English.

We call these wars the French and Indian Wars because the English were fighting both the French **and** the Indians. The wars ended in 1763 when France was finally defeated. England made France give up all of her land in North America.

IROQUOIS DESERVE CREDIT The Iroquois deserve much of the credit for England's victory. If these strong and powerful Indians, with their great knowledge of the woods, had not been on England's side, France might have won. Our lives today would be quite different from what they are, had that happened.

During the time of these wars with the French, the Mohawks became very friendly with a particular white man. He is important in the story of the Iroquois, and we will tell his story here.

Sir William Johnson

Sir William Johnson arrived from Ireland in 1737 when he was just a young man. He had come to look after the land his uncle owned in the Mohawk Valley. William loved the land, and decided he would have some of his own some day. He was also wise enough to know that the best way to get land was to be honest and fair with the Indians who lived on the land.

JOHNSON, THE MOHAWKS' FRIEND William Johnson became the Mohawks' best friend. He learned their language and their customs. Many times he dressed as the Mohawks did. He earned their trust and friendship. In fact, the Mohawks thought so much of this man that he was adopted into the tribe and given an Indian name.

There is a story about the hatchet marks on the stairway in Johnson's home. It is said they were made there by the Mohawks as a sign to all other Indians that this man was never to be harmed. He was always to be protected by the Indians.

Later, the king of England put Johnson in charge of all Indian affairs in New York State. When the wars with the French began, everyone wondered what the mighty Iroquois would do. It was William Johnson who talked the Indians into fighting on the side of England. The fierce and brave Iroquois fighters helped England win the war.

COUNCIL MEETINGS AT JOHNSTOWN The Mohawk held many of their council meetings on the grounds of Sir William's home at Johnstown. There is still a large circle of very old lilac bushes at Johnson Hall, his home. Within the circle the chiefs held their meetings. Each bush represented a chief. Standing within the circle is a tall, beautiful oak tree. The Indians said that the oak was Sir William.

4. From 1763 Until the American Revolution

After the wars with the French were over in 1763, the English and the Indians lived at peace for several years. During this time they made a very, very important treaty (an agreement between nations).

Until this time most of the white settlers in New York had lived along the Hudson and Mohawk Rivers. They had not settled farther west because they were afraid of the Iroquois.

The Iroquois were very happy to trade with the white men, but they did not feel very happy about white families moving in and taking land from the Indians. The Iroquois lived in peace with **each other,** and they were kind and good to their own people. However, they could also be very warlike, savage, and cruel to people they considered their enemies.

The Iroquois did not like the white settlers. In fact, they were considered to be enemies of the Iroquois. Settlers were killed or captured when they tried to settle on Iroquois land.

TREATY OF FT. STANWIX In 1768 the Iroquois and the English signed the Treaty of Fort Stanwix. The treaty gets its name from the place where it was signed. This treaty drew a line running north and south through the state from Fort Stanwix (it is called Rome today) to Deposit. White men were free to settle anywhere east of the line, but **all** the land west of the line was to remain Iroquois land.

The Iroquois promised not to harm any settler who settled east of the line, but all settlers were to stay out of the western lands. This treaty is important because it was the first by which the white men began to get land away from the Indians.

You will read in another chapter about the Iroquois in the American Revolution. After the Revolution, more and more people began to move into the Indian lands. They plowed the land for farms. They built settlements which grew into towns and cities. The Indians tried to keep the white men out but there were too many of them. Little by little the Indians sold most of their land to the white men. In return the United States government set aside several large pieces of land just for the use of the Indians. These lands are called reservations. Most of New York's Indians today live on these reservations.

BOTH SIDES NEED THE INDIANS England sent men to speak to the Iroquois about the war. The colonists also sent men to the Council of the Six Nations to see what part they would take in the war. Each side in the quarrel said the same thing to the Indians. Neither side wanted the Iroquois to be in the war at all.

Both sides knew how savage the Iroquois could be in battle. They were feared by everyone—white men and other Indians alike. The white men wanted the Iroquois to stay at home—to be neutral.

Courtesy of Fenimore House

Gilbert Stuart's Joseph Brant (Thayendanega)

The Oneida tribe thought that being neutral was a good idea, and they decided to remain so. They begged the other five tribes to do the same thing. However, they did not suceed.

JOSEPH BRANT There was a famous Mohawk chief whose English name was Joseph Brant. Brant had been like a son to Sir William Johnson. Even though Sir William was dead, Brant felt he ought to remain loyal to England. Brant said, "I have learned to live as a good subject of the English, and to honor the king. A Mohawk must remain true to his beliefs. He cannot change them." This meant that Brant, the great Captain of the Six Nations, was ready to take all the Iroquois into the war on England's side.

It was decided, however, to let each tribe do as it wished. In the end, the Oneidas and about half of the Tuscaroras stayed out of the war, or fought for the Americans. The Senecas, the Mohawks, the Onondagas, the rest of the Tuscaroras, and the Cayugas fought for England against the American colonists. Altogether, Joseph Brant had an army of about fifteen hundred Iroquois who fought on the side of the British Army.

5. The Treaties

The Americans won their war for Independence from England, and peace was made in 1783. The Indians of New York State had tried to help England win. They should have had some reward for what they did, but England paid very little attention to the Indians after the war was over. The only reward they received was a large piece of land on Grand River in Ontario. Many Indians in the Mohawk and Cayuga tribes moved to this place in Canada. Today there is a beautiful city there named Brantford. Its name was given in honor of Joseph Brant and his family who settled there after the Revolution.

GEORGE WASHINGTON SPEAKS UP FOR THE IROQUOIS What did the Americans do with the Iroquois after peace came? Many people wanted to send all of them out of the country forever. Others felt that this was not right. The Indians had done the things they did because there was a war going on. The Americans had also done some cruel things. War is never nice.

George Washington was one of the important Americans who spoke up for the Iroquois. He knew that the land really belonged to the Indians, and that the white men were the invaders. He believed that the white men needed to be very fair and honest in talking with the Indians about the land. He also believed that the Indians had a right to stay on parts of the land forever. The Iroquois considered George Washington a great man. They admired him so much that he is the only white man who has been allowed in the Iroquois heaven.

A NEW TREATY   The white men of the new United States and the red men of the Iroquois Confederdacy met again in 1784 to sign another treaty. This meeting took place at Fort Stanwix, and like the one before, this treaty was about land. Who should own it? Who should live on it?

This time the white men received a large part of the land of New York State. In this treaty the Iroquois gave up to the United States all of the Indian land west of Buffalo Creek.

During the next six years, the Iroquois signed agreement after agreement, each time giving up to the United States another large piece of land which had been the Indians' for many hundreds of years.

6.   The Big Tree Council

The last big council held by the white men and the Indians was held in 1797 at Big Tree, near Geneseo, New York. The council was held because the white men wanted to buy western New York from the Senecas and Tuscaroras.

The Indians came to the council from miles away. Whole villages packed up and came, because a big council meeting was also a good time to visit! Some books say there were over three thousand Indians at the Big Tree Council.

In the end, the Indians signed the Big Tree Treaty. The Indians received $100,000 for their land. Also, they said they would move to reservations. At this time, too, the Tuscaroras were given two square miles of reservation land.

By 1800 the Iroquois had very little land left in New York State. They had sold almost all of their land to the land agents. The Indians believed they had no right to sell their land, so selling it was not an easy thing for them to do. The earth was their mother, and it was against their religion to think of selling it. However, the white men were powerful, and they used many dishonest ways of getting the Indians to sign the agreements. Soon the Indians lost all of their land except for the few pieces left to them called "reservations."

7. Reservations

A reservation is a piece of land set aside by the government for a special purpose. In the case of the Indian reservations, the land belongs only to the Indians and is not really a part of New York State.

If New Yorkers want to use an Indian reservation for any purpose, they must first ask the Indians who own it. For example, many years ago when the railroads were being built, the

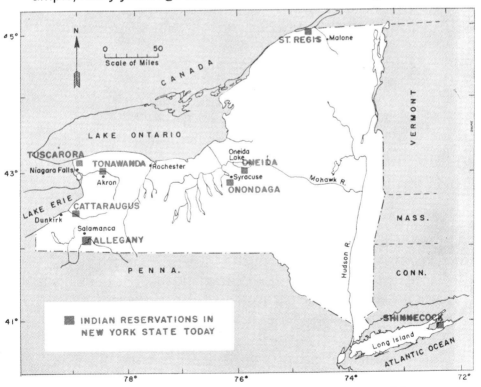

Indian Reservations in New York State today

white people needed some of the Indians' land for their railroads. Enough land was leased, or rented, for the railroads and the towns which grew up beside them.

Today the city of Salamanca and the villages of Vandalia, Killbuck, Carrollton, and Great Valley are located on the land owned by the Senecas. These places must pay a rent to the Senecas every year for the use of the land. Also, if a white person wants to hunt or fish on Indian land, he must buy a license from the Indians who own the land. A New York State hunting or fishing license will not do any good.

Today there are over six thousand Indians in New York State. Almost all of them live in the seven reservations located in different parts of the state.

1. **Onondaga Reservation, near Syracuse**
2. **Allegany Reservation, in the southwestern corner of the state**
3. **Cattaraugus Reservation, near Gowanda, in the western part of the state**
4. **Tuscarora Reservation, near Niagara Falls**
5. **Tonawanda Reservation, near Akron**
6. **St. Regis Reservation, near Hogansburg, on the St. Lawrence River**
7. **Shinnecock Reservation, on Long Island**

The first six reservation listed are Iroquois reservations. The last one is an Algonkian reservation. Some of the reservations are large. Others are quite small. Allegany Reservation, for instance, has over thirty thousand acres of land, but the Shinnecock Reservation has only about four hundred acres—about the area of a good-sized farm.

The Tonawanda, Allegany, and Cattaraugus reservations all belong to the Seneca Indians. The Onondaga Reservation, of course, belongs to the Onondagas. The St. Regis Reservation is a Mohawk reservation.

Neither the Oneida nor the Cayuga Nations have reservations. The Oneida Indians once had a reservation, but they divided it up among themselves many years ago, and they stopped being a tribe. The Cayuga Indians sold all their lands to the white men as long ago as 1807 .There are a few members of both tribes left, and they live with friends on the other reservations.

OTHER INDIAN LANDS   There are two pieces of land still owned by the Indians, although no one lives on either of them. One of them is the Oil Spring Reservation, still owned by the Senecas. The other is the Poosepatuck Reservation on Long Island. The few Poosepatucks who are left nowadays live at Mastic.

More people live on the Cattaraugus Reservation than on any other. The Mohawk reservation at St. Regis is second, while the Allegany reservation is third in the number of people living there. It is interesting to know that the number of Indians in New York State has been getting larger for the past twenty years.

Courtesy of the New York State Department of Commerce
Seneca Indian council house, Letchworth State Park

33

8.   Indian Life Today

Do you wonder what it would be like to live on an Indian reservation? In a great many ways it is not very different from the way people live who do not live on reservations. The houses are very much like the ones seen in any town. Some are poor houses, but most are small, neat frame houses with colorful flower and vegetable gardens. There are a few log cabins here and there, but no one lives in a longhouse.

1. The Modern Longhouse

There is a longhouse, though, on every Iroquois reservation. Today it is used for the religious ceremonies and festivals. It is also the place where the council meets when it is necessary to decide important matters.

The longhouse is a simple, white building, much like a country school or church building. It has two doors, one at each end. One of these is the door through which the men enter the building. The other is for the women to use.

2. Modern Indian Workers

The men and women who live on the reservations earn their living in many ways. They do not have to stay on the reservation, but may work anywhere they choose.

Many men work in the aluminum mills at Massena, and in the steel mills in Buffalo. In fact, the Indians work at almost every trade. Some of them go on to college and learn to be teachers, doctors, lawyers, and scientists. In this way they are no different from other people.

Some of the Mohawks, however, do have a job that is very different. They are the world's greatest experts in working in places high above the ground. They have no fear while working at the very highest places. This means that they can get good jobs building bridges, high buildings, and such things as television towers. Mohawk Indians helped build the Brooklyn Bridge, the George Washington Bridge, the Golden Gate Bridge, and the Empire State Building.

George Washington Bridge

INDIAN SCHOOLS   The children of the Indians go to school just as other American children do, and study the same kinds of things. They are also taught the history, customs, and traditions of their own people. In some places, the school is on the reservation. In other places, the Indian children go to the school nearest them. School buses come to their homes each morning, just as they do for other children in many places through the state.

The Indian child learns English in school, but he probably speaks his Indian language when he is at home. Some of the older people still speak very little English—some speak no English at all.

35

HOLIDAYS   The holidays of Indian children are different from those of other children. On each reservation are held the festivals of which you read earlier. The Maple Sugar Festival is held in the spring; the Festival of the Green Corn in the summer. The boys and girls probably have just as much fun, and eat just as much as their ancestors did hundreds of years ago.

DANCES   Each year, near the end of January, the Midwinter Festival is held in each Iroquois Longhouse. During this festival, the babies are given their Indian names. The old dances, such as the War Dance, the Bear Dance, and the Feather Dance are done. Dreams are told, and the False Face Society appears.

Sometimes, in an Indian home, special dances are held. One of these is the Dark Dance which goes along with the story of the Great Little People.

The Dark Dance is a group of many songs and dances done in the dark. Rattles and drums accompany the dancers. After the dance is over, a feast of corn soup is served by the hostess. When the guests go home, each one takes a pail of corn soup with him.

GAMES   Indian boys and girls play many of the same games other children do. They, too, like baseball and basketball. However, lacrosse is still one of their favorite games.

A visitor to a reservation in the winter would see Indian boys making and playing with snow snakes. Little girls still play with corn husk dolls which their mothers and big sisters make for them.

The Indian boys and girls love sports, particularly racing. Indian children are often the best athletes in their schools.

Council of Six Nations

The Council of the Six Nations still meets each year at Onondaga, where it met in the days before the white man. Here the

Iroquois discuss their problems, and decide what to do about them. No white person is allowed to visit the council meetings.

The chiefs still meet around a council fire. They still pray to the Great Spirit. They still burn sacred tobacco. They may not wear leather clothes, and feathers in their hair, but they are Iroquois just the same!

INDIAN SELF-GOVERNMENT　The Iroquois feel that they are still a nation. Their government is the Council of the Six Nations. However, they never make a rule which is against New York State or United States law. They feel that the agreements made long ago, between their ancestors and the white men, are still good. The Indians feel that both they and the white men should live up to those agreements. Sometimes there are problems that arise.

Often, the white man feels that he has the right to take reservation land away from the Indian. The land is wanted in order to build big power dams or highways. Of course, this also happens to anyone whose land is needed by the public.

The Mohawks lost many acres of land, and many homes were given up when the St. Lawrence Seaway was built. The Indians receive some money when this sort of thing happens, but that does not make up for the loss of land and home.

The Tuscaroras nearly lost a large part of their reservation several years ago. New York State had decided to build a great project which would help to get more power from Niagara Falls.

In order to keep their land, the Tuscaroras had a bitter fight with the New York State Power Authority for over two years. Eventually, the Federal Power Commission decided that the State Power Authority had no right to take the Indians' lands.

The Senecas may lose the best part of their Allegany Reservation soon because of a new dam being planned on the Allegany River. It will be called the Kinzua Dam. The Senecas, too, are fighting hard, through the courts, to save their land.

PERHAPS YOU WOULD LIKE TO . . .

1. Draw a map of New York State which shows the provisions of the Treaty of Fort Stanwix.
2. Make a more detailed report to the class about the French and Indians Wars.
3. Write a report on the life and achievements of Isaac Jogues.
4. Make a wall mural which will show the life of the Indians before and after the white man came.
5. Use your **Richards New York State Atlas** to find out more about the trade empire of the Iroquis. Make a smaller map of this empire for your notebook or bulletin board.
6. Read the story on the Tuscaroras' exciting fight to save their land in the EASTERN WOODLAND INDIANS, Book 2, by Jeanne Schwarz.

THE WONDERFUL WORLD OF WORDS . . .

1. empire   4. missionary   7. language
2. warrior   5. missionaries   8. knight
3. territory   6. ancestors   9. exert

TO HELP YOU REMEMBER . . .

1. In what way did Henry Hudson's visit change the life of the Indians?
2. Why did the Iroquois hate the French?
3. Why were the Iroquois the leaders in the fur trade?
4. Where did the Iroquois get their furs?
5. Give three ways in which the Indian's life changed after the white man came.
6. Who was Isaac Jogues? What did he do? What happened to him?
7. Who was the sixth member of the Iroquois Confederacy?

Chapter III

LIFE IN NEW NETHERLANDS

CHAPTER III

1. The First White Men

GIOVANNI DA VERRAZANO   The very first white man to see the land which we call New York State was an explorer from Italy. He was working for the King of France. His name was Giovanni (Italian for John) da Verrazano. He came in 1524. He only sailed in and out of New York Harbor. Almost a hundred years went by before another white man came.

HENRY HUDSON   That man was Henry Hudson. He was trying to find a shorter way to India and China than was then known. Some men in Holland had paid him to do this. In those days men sailed their ships all the way around Africa to get to India and China. Hudson sailed west across the Atlantic Ocean. This was just as Columbus had done. He found a beautiful harbor and a river which reached far inland. Hudson sailed up this river to the spot where Albany now is. He thought this would be a good place for the Dutch to settle. The Indians were friendly. They wanted to trade furs in return for the white man's goods. The furs could be sold for a great deal of money in Europe. Hudson claimed the land for the King of the Netherlands (another name for Holland).

THE DUTCH WEST INDIA COMPANY   The Dutch merchants agreed with Hudson. These merchants formed the Dutch West India Company. The king gave this company complete charge of the new colony. They called this new colony New Netherlands. The king got part of the money made by the company from the sale of furs.

THE FIRST DUTCH SETTLERS   The first Dutch settlers came in 1624. They built a small fort where Albany now stands. They called this place Fort Orange. Other men settled at the

40

mouth of the river. They called their settlement New Amsterdam. In 1626 Peter Minuit made one of the greatest real estate buys in all history. Peter Minuit was the first governor of the New Netherlands. For about $24 worth of trinkets he bought the island of Manna-hatta from the Algonkian Indians. That island is our Manhattan Island. It is one of the richest pieces of property in the whole world.

2. New Netherlands Grows Slowly

LIFE IS HARDER IN THE NEW COLONY   The colony of New Netherlands grew very slowly. It is no wonder! Life was very hard. Very few people would leave a comfortable home in Holland to live in the wilderness. To get people to come the company paid the fare over to the new world. In return, the company made settlers do certain things. The company owned all of the land. They did not let each settler own his own farm.

Dutch land owner and tenant

41

The company gave the farmers seeds and some cows when they arrived. In return, for many years the settlers had to give the company first choice when it was time to sell their crops. They had to give the company half of all the calves that were born **and** they had to buy all of their supplies from the company. They had to pay whatever price the company wanted to charge.

THE PATROONSHIPS The Dutch West India Company tried to think of new ways to get people to live in their colony. One of these ways was the patroon system. The company gave large pieces of land to any man who would bring fifty or more settlers to the colony. The man was called a patroon. The land he owned was a patroonship. The settlers who came worked for the patroon. They gave him a share of all they raised. He gave them a house and seeds and animals. It was much like life in the Middle Ages.

3. People Who Lived in New Netherlands

PEOPLE CAME FROM MANY COUNTRIES The people who lived in New Netherlands came from many countries. Some were German and some were French; many others were English. Swedish people came also, and Negroes and Jews and Scots. Indeed, at one time over eighteen different languages could be heard on Manhattan Island. It is still that way, isn't it? These people lived mainly in large settlements. New Amsterdam was the largest of these. In 1664 it had 350 houses and about 1,500 people. They had a fort with about 70 soldiers. There was a house for the governor, a school, and the Dutch Reformed Church.

THE FLUSHING REMONSTRANCE Many of these people had been treated badly in their own countries because of their religion. They thought they would find freedom of worship in the New World. However, it did not work out that way. For instance, one time, in 1657, Governor Peter Stuyvesant gave this order — any person who allowed a Quaker to stay in his house overnight would have to pay a fine. The English people of Flushing, on Long Island, did not like this. They wrote an answer to the governor. This answer is called the Flushing Remonstrance. This was the very first time that just plain people spoke out for religious tolerance. Today we believe that everyone has the right to worship in his own way. The Flushing Remonstrance helped us to get this right.

Stuyvesant surrenders to the English

4. The English Take Over

During these years many English settlers came into New Netherlands. Some came straight from England. Others came from the English colonies of Massachusetts and Connecticut. In 1664 England decided that she would take the rich fur trading colony for her own. England was then at war with Holland. This gave her an excuse to send warships into the New York Harbor.

The English captain had four ships, sixty-two guns, and 400 soldiers. He demanded that the Dutch surrender. Peter Stuyvesant was governor at that time and he refused to surrender. Still, he had only twenty guns and seventy soldiers. He held out against the English for a week but then he had to give up. The fort was not strong enough to stand up against English guns. Then, too, the people of New Amsterdam didn't really care. Peter Stuyvesant was a very stern governor. He made life in New Netherlands very hard. The people in New Amsterdam felt that things could be no worse under English rule, so the English took over without firing a shot.

HERITAGE FROM THE DUTCH   New Netherlands lasted for only fifty-five years. During that time the Dutch people brought to the New World things and ideas which are part of our lives today.

Do you like cookies? Thank the good Dutch mothers who baked them first. They also taught us to eat crullers and that good cabbage dish which they called coleslaw. Do you think ice-skating is fun? So did the Dutch boys and girls who brought their ice-skates from Holland, the land of canals. Another lovely gift from the Dutch is our celebration of Christmas as a happy gift-giving time. For them December 6 was the magic day when the Dutch boys and girls put out their wooden shoes and waited to see what would happen.

Some of the most interesting things which the Dutch gave to us are the names of places. The word "kill" in the Dutch language means "creek". You will find many places in the lower Hudson area and the Mohawk region with this word in their names. Catskill is an example and so is Cobleskill. Can you think of others or find others on the map of New York? "Wyck" was the Dutch word for "town". In fact, the city of Albany was called Bever**wyck** during the Dutch days. Can you find places on the map which have **wyck** as part of their names? The Dutch also left us certain words which we say all the time. "Boss" is a good example.

Rip Van Winkle, one of the folklore characters we love most, also comes from our Dutch settlers. So do Ichabod Crane, the Headless Horseman and Katrina Van Tassel whom you will meet in **The Legend of Sleepy Hollow** by Washington Irving. The Dutch truly helped to make New York's history rich and interesting.

TO HELP YOU REMEMBER . . .

1. Who was the first white man to visit New York?

2. When did Henry Hudson come to New York? Why did he come? Why did he think New York was a good place?

3. Who had charge of the new colony?

4. Who were the first settlers in the new colony? Why did they come?

5. Why is Peter Minuit famous?

6. Why did New Netherlands grow slowly?

7. What kinds of people lived in New Netherlands?

8. What was the Flushing Remonstrance? Why is it important?

9. Who was Peter Stuyvesant?

10. What happened to New Netherlands in 1664?

PERHAPS YOU WOULD LIKE TO . . .

1. Pretend you are working for the Dutch West India Company. Make posters advertising New Netherlands and trying to get people to settle there.

2. Write a report on Rensselaerswyck, the successful patroonship. You can find information about it in **A Short History of New York.** Your librarian may suggest other books.

3. Look up more details on the Flushing Remonstrance and write a report on it.

Chapter IV

LIFE IN EARLY NEW YORK

1. The Settlers
2. Pioneer Life

CHAPTER IV

1. THE SETTLERS

The first thing the English did was to change the name of the colony. The King of England gave the colony to his brother, the Duke of York. New Amsterdam was changed to New York. Two other settlements became Albany and Kingston. For over one hundred years New York was an English colony. Let's take a good look at those years in the next few pages.

WHERE THE SETTLERS LIVED   First of all, where did the people live during those years? Most of the villages and farms were along the Hudson River and on Long Island. A few very brave people lived as far away as Schenectady. Others lived in the valley of the Mohawk River. Still others were people on farms and tiny settlements in Schoharie County. This was frontier country. Frontier means the farthest edge of settlement. The wilderness comes after the frontier. Most of the people hugged the shores of the Hudson. They feared the Mohawk Indians who lived to the north and west of them. There were very few people in the central and western part of New York State until after the Revolutionary War.

THE SETTLERS   People continued to come to New York State. There were a number of different groups. In 1678 twelve brave French families settled at New Paltz. In 1713, 150 German families came into the Schorarie Valley. They were called Palatines. Another group who helped settle the frontier in New York were the Scotch-Irish, who settled in Cherry Valley.

THE PALATINES SETTLE   These people have a very interesting story. For many years they had lived along the Rhine River in Germany. When the French king and his armies marched over Germany in war, these people were driven from their homes. They went to London, the great city of England, and tried to settle down there and make new homes. However, the English king did not want them there and he decided to send them to America.

The English navy needed pitch and tar and masts for their ships. The English government said they would give the Germans homes and food in New York if they would make these things for the navy. The English set up two camps for the German people. One was at Germantown and one at West Camp.

The Germans came but the plan did not work. The English did not keep their promises and the Germans did not like the work they had to do. The plan was given up and the Germans had to find homes for themselves.

The Palatines working to produce naval stores

They went first to the Schoharie Valley where they cleared land and built houses. Then they were told that they would have to pay for the land or get off. Some of them paid and stayed on their farms. Others went away to Pennsylvania where land was cheaper. Most of them moved to the Mohawk River. The governor gave them free land where Palatine Bridge and Stone Arabia are now. A few years later more Germans came and settled further west, where Herkimer now stands.

HOW THE LAND WAS DIVIDED   The governor of the colony, who was appointed by the king, had the right to give away or sell the land. He was supposed to give most of this money to the king. Sometimes a governor gave very large pieces of land to his friends. The largest pieces of land were called manors. A man who owned a manor was called "lord of the manor." His word was law. The people who had farms on the manor did not really own them. They were called tenants. They had to pay the lord of the manor a certain rent every year in cash. Also, they had to give him something from the farm. For instance, it might be four fat hens and one day's work with horse and oxen each year. If a man "sold" his land, he had to give the lord of the manor one quarter of the price. The people did not like this way of living. They wanted to own their own land and work for themselves. It was often hard to pay the rent. Many times they refused to pay the rent. There were some very exciting days in the Hudson Valley. If you would like to read about them, get the book called "Rebellion at Quaker Hill" by Carl Carmer, and read the story of Will Prendergast.

Rebellion at Quaker Hill

THE LAND SPECULATORS APPEAR The governors of the colony also granted land to men called land speculators. A land speculator is a man who buys land at a cheap price. Then he sells it at a higher price. This is how most of the early settlers got their land. They bought it from land companies or land speculators who first got it in a grant from a governor.

2. PIONEER LIFE

LIFE ON THE FARM Farmers grew their own food and the food for people in the cities and villages too. The pioneer farmer made everything else he and his family needed. He built his own house and barns. He made his own tools most of the time.

The farm wife grew her own flax and spun her own thread. Then she wove her own cloth. She made her own soap and candles. Life was hard for a pioneer farm family. Everyone, even the children, worked from morning to night. Girls learned to spin when they were very young. Even the boys learned to clean and "card" the sheep's wool. Then their mothers and sisters could spin it into yarn. Children helped in the fields and in the barns. Every hand was needed.

There was fun, too, on a pioneer farm. "Harvestime" was exciting. Maple "sugartime" was always a good time. There were wonderful stories to tell and be heard in front of a winter's fire. There were husking bees and quilting bees. These were times when neighbors gathered for work and fun together.

Some things the farmer grew could be sold for cash. These things were called "cash crops." With this money they could

Sleigh, 1761

buy things they could not grow or make, things like salt and sugar and tea. New York grew so much wheat that they had some to sell the people in the other colonies. Another cash crop was beef and pork. Another thing the farmer sold for money was potash made from the trees on his farm.

CRAFTS AND SKILLS   Not everyone lived on a farm, of course. There were cities and villages and people there made their living in many ways. Let's see how many ways we can think of.

The first kind of mill in any community was usually a grist mill or a saw mill. The grist mill turned the farmer's wheat into flour and his corn into cornmeal. The saw mill turned the farmer's trees into smooth lumber which could be made into better houses and beautiful tables, chairs and beds. There were many grist mills and saw mills in colonial times. The cooper was also an important man. He made staves for barrels.

There were also very skilled men who made shingles for houses and masts and spars for ships. Some men made their living in the tanning business, turning animal skins into good leather.

The bark of the hemlock tree was important for this so tanning was a big business in the Catskill Mountains because there were so many hemlock trees there.

There was an iron industry in the Hudson Valley during colonial times. The largest mine was at Ancram. This was where they made the famous chain which went across the Hudson River during the Revolution. There is a picture of this chain in this book.

Many men in colonial days were skilled craftsmen. This means they could do one thing and do it very, very well. There were glassblowers and wigmakers, and men who made fine furniture. There were chandlers who made candles, and gunsmiths, and hatters. Finally there was the blacksmith who made shoes for the horses and oxen and also many tools for use in the house and on the farm.

Some of the people in the colonies made a living by keeping inns where people could eat and stay overnight. These inns often were used for other things, too, such as dances, and as places for a judge to hold court.

THE TRADERS   Many people, especially in New York City and Albany, made a living by trading. They sold furs and potash to England. They also traded with people in the West Indies who needed food and lumber. In return they received cotton and spices and sugar from the West Indies. Then the New York traders sold these things to England. In return they received iron products and cloth. The trade made a triangle between New York, the West Indies and England. It also made a great many people very rich, because the men in New York were very good businessmen.

CHURCHES IN COLONIAL NEW YORK   In some of the thirteen colonies only one church was allowed and everyone had to belong to it. This was not true in New York. Yorkers did not have to belong to any church. If they wanted to go to church, there were several to choose from.

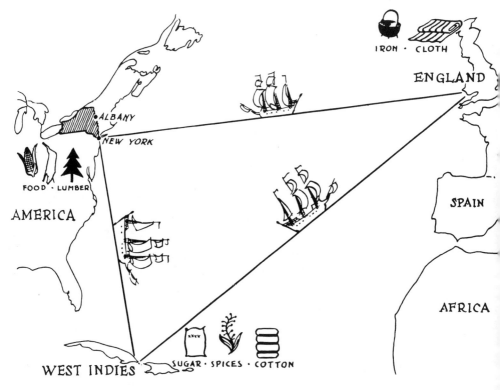

The triangle of trade

SCHOOLS IN COLONIAL NEW YORK   There were not very many schools in colonial New York. Schools were started by the churches in order to teach boys and girls how to read the Bible. The churches also needed schools to train young men to become ministers in the church. In colonial days families had to pay a sum of money for each child who went to school. This money is called "tu-i-tion." Many families were too poor to pay the tuition so more than half of the boys and girls did not go to school. Most of those who did go to school went only for the first few grades. They learned only how to read and write and do simple arithmetic.

54

Rich people often had a **tutor** teach their children. A tutor is a private teacher who teaches in the home, not in a school. Only the rich boys went to college. They could go to King's College in New York City (now Columbia University) or to Yale College in Connecticut, Harvard College in Massachusetts, or Princeton College in New Jersey. Girls didn't go to college at all. In fact, very few girls went to any kind of school. Girls were taught how to sew and cook and keep house. Their mothers were their teachers. Girls from rich families often had extra lessons in manners and dancing and the French language. Things were very different then from the way they are now.

THE DISPUTED EASTCHESTER ELECTION ~ 1733

lection held October 29, 1733, on the Eastchester green to choose a representative to the New ovincial assembly, public resentment against or Cosby was expressed by the overwhelming y vote cast for Lewis Morris, whom the Governor charged as Chief Justice. Attempting unsuccessfully to change the election result, the royal Sheriff ordered a second balloting during which he denied the vote to thirty-seven Quakers who had previously voted for Morris.

This action added to the general discontent which led John Peter Zenger to found the *New-York Weekly Journal*.

Courtesy of the New York State Department of Commerce
"*The Disputed Eastchester Election*"

TO HELP YOU REMEMBER . . .

1. What changes did the English make when they took over the colony?
2. Where did most of the people live in the late 1600's?
3. What does frontier mean? Where was the frontier?
4. Who settled New Paltz?
5. Who were the Palatines? In what part of New York did they settle?
6. What was a manor?
7. What was a land speculator?
8. What was a "cash crop"? Give an example.
9. Make a list of other ways of making a living during colonial days besides farming.
10. What is meant by the term "triangle trade"?
11. Who went to school during colonial days? What did they learn in school?

WONDERFUL WORLD OF WORDS . . .

1. frontier
2. ancestors
3. manor
4. tenant
5. speculator
6. flax
7. potash
8. fertilizer
9. cooper
10. triangle

PERHAPS YOU WOULD LIKE TO . . .

1. Take a trip to Cooperstown where you can really see flax spun into thread and then woven into cloth. There are many other things to see there, things which tell you about pioneer life in New York State.
2. Make models of the various ways of making a living mentioned in the chapter. If, however, you don't have room to make or display these, you could make a group of posters showing the many skills you have read about.
3. Make a poster of the triangle trade.
4. Pretend that you are a pioneer boy or girl and keep a diary for a week. Tell all that you do and see and think.
5. Pretend that you are a Palatine German. Write a letter back home telling of your experiences in the New World.

Chapter V

DEMOCRACY GROWS IN NEW YORK

57

CHAPTER V

1. The Beginning of Democracy

OUR KIND OF GOVERNMENT   You have heard for many years that we live in a democracy in the United States. Do you know what this means? It means that in our country we have government to do the things for our citizens which we cannot do as well ourselves. Government serves the people. Democracy means, too, that government is run by the people of the state or the country. In some countries it is the other way around — the people are run by the government. The people serve the government. Democracy is a kind of government in which the people have power. We are proud of our kind of government. We think that it is the best way for people to live.

Such a government as ours has not happened easily or quickly. It had to grow and many people had to work hard. Some of them had to suffer and die so that democracy could grow stronger and stronger. Democracy is still growing and will grow stronger as long as we, too, are willing to work hard to help. This chapter will tell you some of the stories of how democracy began in New York State. All of the stories will be about the time when New York was a colony.

2. The First English Governors

During the years when the Dutch had control of our state there was no democracy at all. The Dutch West India Company ruled the colony with an iron hand. The people had no say in what happened. There was no trial by jury. When Peter Stuyvesant was governor there was very little freedom of religion.

THE DUKE'S LAWS   When the English took over the colony in 1664 things began to be a little better. The first governor sent over by the Duke of York was Robert Nicolls. Governor Nicolls was a good man. He wanted the people of the colony to have as many rights as possible. He called a group of them together at Hempstead, Long Island. There they wrote out a list of rights which they called the Duke's Laws. They named them this because the Duke of York approved of them. These laws said that all colonists would have freedom of religion and the right to a fair trial by jury. Not only that, but all town governments should be elected by the people who lived in the towns. These were good laws and were the first steps which New York took toward real democracy.

GOVERNOR DONGAN'S ASSEMBLY   Not many years later another governor, Governor Dongan, took another big step toward democracy. He called for representatives of various parts of the colony to meet with him in Albany as an Assembly to discuss the rights of the people. At this meeting they decided to have an Assembly elected by freeholders and freemen. This Assembly would discuss the problems of the people and decide what to do about them. This was the very beginning of the legislature which we have today. We still call the larger part of our legislature the Assembly. Governor Dongan's Assembly, back in 1683, also said that New Yorkers should have freedom of religion and the right to trial by jury.

3. Jacob Leisler — Leisler's Rebellion

The King of England died and his brother, the Duke of York, became king. From that time on he was known as King James II. After he became king, James II seemed to forget all the promises he had made when he was Duke of York. For instance, he would not let the New York Assembly meet. He decided to join New York with New Jersey and New England and make one big colony of them. The man he put in charge of the new colony was Governor Edmund Andros. This man was disliked by everyone. No one liked the new big colony, either. In fact, this was a very unhappy time for all the colonists.

KING JAMES IS FORCED FROM HIS THRONE   The people in England were unhappy, too. They finally forced James II to leave his throne. The people would not have him for their king. When the colonists heard this they were overjoyed! In Boston the first thing they did was to put Governor Andros in jail. When this news reached New York City the citizens took up arms and decided they would choose their own leader. They were tired of being ordered about by a small group of rich merchants and large landowners. They wanted their Assembly back again. They wanted some of the hard laws taken away.

LEISLER ACCEPTS A DANGEROUS POSITION   Their leader was a man named Jacob Leisler and this time in New York's history is called Leisler's Rebellion. Jacob Leisler was one of the richest merchants in the colony but he believed in the same things most of the citizens did. He, too, believed in having an Assembly. He did not believe that a few men should have complete control of the rich trade of New York. These are the reasons why the citizens asked him to take charge of the colony and act as governor until England sent over a new one. Many people believed that he would do a good job and he did.

LEISLER RESTORES THE LAW   The first thing he did was to bring back the New York Assembly so that the people could make their own laws once again. One of the laws the Assembly passed said that there should be no more monopolies in trade. Just in case that is a new word for you, here is what it means. To have a monopoly means to have complete control of something. Governor Andros had given the rich merchants of Albany a monoply on the fur trade. He had given the rich merchants of New York City a monopoly on all trade with foreign countries. All goods coming from a foreign country or going to a foreign country had to be loaded or unloaded at New York City. The trade up and down the Hudson River was only for the freemen

Leisler is led to his doom

of New York City. Other merchants in other towns did not think these laws were fair. That is why the Assembly said there should be no monopolies. The rich merchants of Albany and New York City, of course, did not like the new law. They blamed Jacob Leisler for it. They became his enemies and planned to get even with him some day.

JUSTICE MISCARRIED   After England got a new king and queen, a new governor was sent to New York. Leisler's enemies made friends with the new governor. Soon they saw to it that Leisler was arrested for treason and thrown into jail. Leisler was not given a fair trial because all of the people who judged him were on the side of his enemies. He was found guilty, of course, and was hanged. Jacob Leisler was not a traitor. He was often hot-tempered and he made many people angry. Perhaps he made some mistakes, but he also helped democracy to grow in New York.

LEISLER'S SACRIFICE NOT IN VAIN   After Leisler died, the new governor let the Assembly go on meeting. This Assembly was elected by the freemen of the colony. As the years went on, the Assembly grew stronger and stronger. By 1737, the Assembly had complete control over the tax money of the colony. The governors had been forced to give up this power to the people. This was another big step in the growth of democracy.

4. John Peter Zenger

One of the most thrilling stories about democracy in New York State is the one about a poor printer named John Peter Zenger. Here is the story.

GOVERNOR COSBY ARRIVES   The king appointed a man named Cosby to be governor of New York. Cosby did not go to New York for many months. Another man, Rip Van Dam, had to act as governor until he got there. When Cosby arrived he decided he would like to have half of the salary which had been paid to the acting governor. Naturally, Mr. Van Dam refused. Governor Cosby then sued Van Dam! In order to win his case, the governor started a new court.

This new court was in charge of a judge who was a friend of his. The Chief Justice of New York (the highest judge) was a man named Lewis Morris. Judge Morris told the governor that he had no right to start the new court. The governor was very angry and fired Mr. Morris! This did not make Mr. Morris very happy. He and his friends decided to do something about it. They asked John Peter Zenger, a poor printer, if he would publish a newspaper which would tell the people the truth about the dishonesty of Governor Cosby. Zenger agreed and the **Weekly Journal** began to appear.

GOVERNOR COSBY NOT DEMOCRATIC   In the newspaper were stories and articles which told the people how dishonest their governor really was. They didn't always use the governor's name, but everyone knew who the stories were about. When the governor saw the paper you can imagine how he felt and how he acted. Probably his fist shook and his face turned purple, he was so angry! Finally, he gave orders that all copies of the **Weekly Journal** should be burned! Next, he ordered his officers to arrest John Peter Zenger, the little man who had dared to print the newspaper!

Courtesy of the New York State Department of Commerce
Zenger Memorial, Sub-Treasury Building, New York City

ZENGER IS CHARGED UNJUSTLY   The charge placed against Zenger was "seditious libel." Those are two new, hard words and here is what they mean. Libel means a written untruth which will hurt a person's reputation. We have laws against libel today. You cannot say anything about a person which is both untrue and hurtful to his reputation or character. If you do, that person can sue you. "Seditious" (see-dish-us) libel is an untruth which will stir up the people against the government and get them to revolt. This is what Governor Cosby said Peter Zenger had done in his newspaper — printed untrue things which would stir up the people of New York against the king's government. This was a very serious charge. It could mean Zenger's death!

63

ZENGER REMAINS IN JAIL FOR SIX MONTHS   Zenger stayed in jail for more than six months without a trial. However, he was never afraid, and, somehow, the **Weekly Journal** kept right on appearing even though he was in jail. The officers allowed Zenger's wife to visit him once a week and talk to him for a few minutes through a hole in the door. During those minutes Zenger whispered to her and told her what to do. Then she would see that the paper was printed. She was brave, too!

Courtesy of the New York State Department of Commerce
"Zenger's Wife Visits Him in Jail."—Zenger Memorial

The governor refused to let Zenger have his own lawyer to defend him. As the time drew near for the trial, the governor felt sure that he would win because the judge was on his side. He thought the judge could make the jury do what he wanted it to do. Almost everyone agreed with the governor that poor Zenger did not have a chance. He would surely be found guilty and be hanged. What a surprise was in store for everyone, including John Peter Zenger himself!

Courtesy of the New York State Department of Commerce

Andrew Hamilton

ANDREW HAMILTON ARRIVES TO SAVE THE DAY Just as the trial was almost over, the door of the courtroom was thrown open and there stood Andrew Hamilton, the greatest lawyer in all the colonies. He was an old man and not very well, but he had taken the rough ride in a stagecoach all the way from Philadelphia to New York City to defend this poor man. He even refused to take any money for what he did. The reason is not hard to find.

He believed that something very important to all people was being decided at that trial. He told the jury what he thought in a wonderful speech which lasted many hours. He told them **they** must decide if Zenger had printed the **truth;** if he had, then they must free him. Men must be able to speak and print the truth if they were to be free men and not slaves. The jury listened closely to what the great lawyer said. When he had finished, it took them only a few minutes to decide that Zenger had printed the truth and was not guilty of seditious libel. The trial made John Peter Zenger a free man. It also was the first big step toward the freedom of the press which we have today.

TO HELP YOU REMEMBER . . .

1. Who has the power in a democratic government?
2. What is the purpose of government in a democracy?
3. How much democracy was there in New Netherland?
4. Make a list of the Duke's Laws. You should have three.
5. When did our state legislature begin?
6. Why did the people of New York rebel after James II left the throne?
7. Who was Jacob Leisler?
8. What did Jacob Leisler do for the citizens of New York?
9. Who were Jacob Leisler's enemies? What did they do to Leisler?
10. Who was John Peter Zenger? Why did he become famous?

THE WONDERFUL WORLD OF WORDS . . .

1. democracy
2. government
3. representative
4. assembly
5. legislature
6. monopoly
7. rebellion
8. treason
9. seditious

PERHAPS YOU WOULD LIKE TO . . .

1. Start a chart called Steps to Democracy. Put on it all the steps you read about in this chapter. You could draw a real stairway with Democracy standing at the top. Or you could have a road, with Democracy at the end. Each step could be a milestone on the Road to Democracy.
2. Make a play out of the story of John Peter Zenger and act it in front of your class.
3. Write a letter to the editor of the newspaper defending Jacob Leisler. In your letter tell what Leisler did for the people of New York and why you do **not** think he is a traitor.
4. Make a poster listing the Duke's Laws. This would be a good chance to practice your skill at lettering.

Chapter VI

THE COLONIAL WARS IN NEW YORK

CHAPTER VI

1. Reasons for the Colonial Wars

THE IMPORTANCE OF NEW YORK STATE'S LOCATION
The next part of New York's story is very important and exciting. It is full of war and terror, of Indian raids and brave men. It is the story of how two great countries, France and England, tried to get control of all of North America and its great riches. What happened back there in those long ago days has real meaning for us today. Why, we might all be speaking French instead of English! New Yorkers played a big and important part in the wars between France and England.

England and France fighting

To understand why you must look at the map and review some of the geography you have already learned. The secret of New York's great importance is in its location. Do you see how it lies between two great areas of water, the Atlantic Ocean and the Great Lakes? Do you see, too, how another great waterway to the west can be reached through New York State?

68

In those days there were no roads, railroads or airplanes. The French were in Canada. The only way they could reach the Ohio River, which leads into the mighty Mississippi River, was to go through New York State. Notice, too, that New York lies between all the other English colonies. Pennsylvania, New Jersey and all the southern colonies are on one side. All the New England colonies are on the other.

Think how good it would be for France if she could control New York. She would have its wonderful harbor and excellent rivers and lakes. With these she could reach far inland and control all the rich fur trade with the far away Indians. She would also be able to divide the English colonies. This would make them easier to defeat. In a short while she would have control of all of the colonies. This is what France thought.

The English were afraid of this, also. The English did not intend to give up New York. They, too, wanted the riches of the far away furs which the Iroquois Indians brought to Albany. They would not give up their water routes easily. They also did not intend to give up their beautiful harbor at New York City. From this harbor they could trade with all the nations of the world, and especially with the rich islands of the West Indies. Look at your map again to see how close that really is.

The wars which came were no surprise to anyone. Each side knew what it wanted. Each side was willing to go to war to get what it wanted.

The English and the French fought four wars with each other in seventy-four years before one side finally gave in. The names of these wars were: King William's War (1689-1697), Queen Anne's War (1701-1713), King George's War (1744-1748) and the famous French and Indian War which lasted from 1754 until 1763.

These were years of great trouble for the people who lived in New York. Time after time their villages and forts were raided and burned by the French and Indians from the north. Their ships were attacked by the French navy and many, many brave men lost their lives.

The Indians were of great importance during these wars. Each side needed to have Indians fighting for them. They knew the ways of the forests. They knew how to fight in the wilderness. They were brave and skillful warriors. The Indians, too, needed the fur trade because they had become used to the white man's goods which could only be bought with furs. They had to decide which side to fight for in order to make sure the rich trade would go on. As we have read, the Hurons and Algonkians fought on the side of the French. Most of the Iroquois, especially the Mohawks, fought on the side of the English.

2. King William's War

The first of the colonial wars was King William's War which lasted from 1689 to 1697. Three things to remember about this war are:

(1) the Schenectady Massacre
(2) the unsuccessful plan to invade Canada, and
(3) the activities of the French leader, Frontenac.

The whole thing began in the spring of 1689 when the Iroquois set out for Canada on a raiding party. Two years before a Frenchman named Denonville had hurt the Senecas very badly. The Iroquois were determined to get even. They went down the St. Lawrence River until they reached Lachine, just a few miles from Montreal. Here there was a terrible massacre. A massacre is the killing of many people at one time. This massacre was so awful that all of Canada was scared of what might happen next.

What did happen next was really frightful. Frontenac sent out French soldiers and Indians to attack forts in New York. They had orders to strike at the heart of New York which was Albany. However, it was February and the snow lay waist deep everywhere. It was bitter cold and the going on snowshoes was hard. As they made camp that night, the men decided

70

The burning of Schenectady

they would leave Albany alone. They would strike out for Schenectady because it was nearer. So, on a cold February night in 1690, Algonkians crept up to the tiny stockaded settlement of Schenectady. This settlement felt so secure that they had left only two snowmen guarding the gate to the stockade. As these silent watchmen stood by, the Indians swept into the village, torches in one hand and murderous tomahawks in the other. The happy, secure Dutchmen, safely asleep in their snug beds, awoke to a night of horror. The air was filled with the screams of the frightened and dying people. The crackle of flames added to the noise as the houses burned to the ground. When the dreadful night was over, only two houses were left standing. Only a few sad men and women were left to look upon the ruins.

The English thought they must fight back after the attack on Schenectady. In August a small army of New Yorkers set out to take Canada. The leader of the army quit when they had reached Lake Champlain. However, John Schuyler (son of Peter Schuyler) took a small group and went on. They did not succeed in taking Canada, but they struck a crippling blow at the settlement of La Prairie. The next year, 1691, John's father, Peter Schuyler, led another small army which struck La Prairie once again. Peter Schuyler was a man of great courage and determination. He was also a great friend of the Iroquois. At this time, he had more influence on the Iroquois than anyone else.

In 1693 Frontenac's French soldiers and Huron Indians reached the Mohawk River. They burned all of the Indian villages. Peter Schuyler tried to rescue his Indian friends but the French came and went too swiftly. In 1696, Frontenac struck again. This time he gathered an army of 2,200 men, a tremendous army for those days. They crossed Lake Ontario and then went to the foot of Lake Onondaga. From there they marched to the Onondaga castle (or village) near the modern village of Jamesville. The Onondagas saw the army coming and knew there was only one thing left to do. They put the torch to their village themselves and then melted quickly and quietly into the nearby forests. When the army arrived it could only burn the crops which were still standing. Everything else was gone, including the Indians.

The next year England and France reached an agreement and signed a treaty of peace. King William's War was over.

3. Queen Anne's War

The treaty signed in 1697 proved to be only a truce. A truce is a temporary stop in an argument or war. It is a waiting period. This truce was broken in 1702 when England and France again began fighting each other.

In Europe this war lasted for eleven years between France and England. It was much shorter than that for their colonies in North America. The French in Canada and the Iroquois and English in New York had taken a good long look at each other after King William's War and decided several things:

The French and Yorkers agree not to fight.

1. The French decided they would not destroy the Iroquois. They decided, instead, to try to get along with them. Then they could keep the lines of communication with their Mississippi Valley settlements open. The furs which the Iroquois took to Albany were of less value than a peaceful Great Lakes region. These lakes were the door leading into the rich Mississippi Valley.

2. The Iroquois had been badly hurt by the French and now had a healthy respect for them. They began to wonder if they had not better join these people instead of fighting them.

3. The Albany and New York City traders had decided that war ruined their business and that it would be much better to get along with the French than to fight them.

These thoughts led the French and the New Yorkers to make an agreement with each other. No matter how much the mother countries fought in Europe, they would not fight each other. The French traders agreed to buy trading goods from the manufacturers in New York, a plan which gave profits to both sides. Because of this agreement, New York was at peace during the first half of Queen Anne's War.

Then England decided that she would try again to conquer Canada. The colonies did not like the idea; they remembered how they had failed before. They also remembered how much money these failures had cost. This time, however, England said that she would pay all the expenses. She also said that the great English navy would come and help. The colonies finally agreed to try again to take Canada away from the French. During the next three years several attempts were made. None of them was successful. The French and the New Yorkers went back to their earlier agreement in 1711 and two years later Queen Anne's War came to an end.

4. King George's War

The story of King George's War is very short. The war lasted only four years and, in North America at least, it was mostly talk. There was no action for the English in New York. The French did come down and burn the village of Saratoga, but that is all. There were big plans made to take Canada but they were never carried out. King George's War made no changes in anything in the New World. The English had missed a good chance to conquer Canada because they could not make up their minds about what to do. The French had discovered that they needed more forts and set about building them.

5. The French and Indian War

The French and Indian War was the last of the colonial wars and the most important of all. It really began in 1754, but all of the action that year took place in Virginia. The main thing which happened in New York in 1754 was a meeting in Albany of delegates from all the colonies. They met to discuss how they could unite to defend themselves against the French. This group accepted a plan written by Benjamin Franklin. The plan was called the Albany Plan of Union. However, when the delegates returned home they found that the colonies would not accept the plan. The plan is very important in our history because it was the first time the colonists had ever even talked about joining with each other for any reason.

Benjamin Franklin's Plan of the Union

In 1755 the English sent William Johnson to take the fort of Crown Point away from the French. You have already read about this man and his influence on the Mohawk Indians. When Johnson reached the carrying-place between the Hudson River and Lake George, he stopped and built a fort which he named Fort Edward. When it was finished, he moved on to the head of the lake and built another fort which he named Fort William Henry in honor of the two grandsons of King George II. The general who was in charge of Crown Point was Baron Dieskau (Dees-kow). Naturally, he was told about Johnson by his scouts. Certainly he didn't like the idea of the enemy settling down in a fort so close to his.

He and his men moved very quickly and surprised a group of English soldiers working near the fort. The very bitter Battle of Lake George was the result. Both generals were wounded. Baron Dieskau died from his wounds. Johnson drove the French back to Fort Carillon (later named Ticonderoga). However, there was now no hope that Johnson could go on and take Crown Point. The French remained where they were. The Battle of Lake George had two results:

Oh! Oh; Here we go again—the agreement is forgotten.

(1) the name of the lake was changed from Lac du St. Sacrament to Lake George in honor of George II, and

(2) William Johnson was made a knight and became **Sir** William Johnson.

The first three years of the French and Indian War belong to the French. The English did not take their forts at Crown Point, Carillon or Niagara. However, the English lost their forts at Oswego and Ontario to the great French general, Montcalm. Fort William Henry also fell to Montcalm in a terrible massacre. The village of German Flats was completely burned by the French.

In 1757 a new man became head of the government in England and took charge of all the military affairs in North America. This man's name was William Pitt. He was young, he was full of confidence, he was afraid of no one. He made great changes so that England could begin to win again. He appointed new generals, the best he could find. He told America that England would pay for the war if the colonists would help by fighting. Enlistments went up and England began to fight back!

General Amherst and General Wolfe took Louisbourg, a fortress in Nova Scotia, away from the French. Colonel Bradstreet destroyed Fort Frontenac and tons of supplies which the French needed very badly. General Amherst forced the French to blow up Fort Carillon and he captured Crown Point. In 1759 Fort Niagara fell to an English force headed by General Predeaux and Sir William Johnson. Then, in September of 1759, the Battle of Quebec took place. This is one of the most historic battles in the history of the world. General James Wolfe was the English leader. His aim was to take Quebec, the capital of New France, away from the French. General Montcalm defended Quebec. The battle took place on the Plains of Abraham, overlooking the city. Both brave generals died in the battle, each believing that he had won.

The English won the Battle of Quebec. The capital city of the French was now gone. The forts, which had once been so proud, were all either destroyed or in the hands of the English. The city of Montreal was all that was left to the French. In 1760 that city, too, surrendered. The colonial wars were over at last!

Three years later, in 1763, men from England and France met in Paris to sign the treaty which ended the war officially. In this treaty France agreed to give up her claims to land in the New World east of the Mississippi River. From that time on the English would control all of North America east of the Mississippi with the exception of Florida and the city of New Orleans. The French would never again be strong in America except for New Orleans and a very small part of Canada. The pattern for our lives was made in that treaty in 1763. If the French had won, we would all be speaking French today as our native language.

TO HELP YOU REMEMBER . . .
1. Why did the French and the English go to war with each other four times?
2. Why did both France and England want the Indians on their side?
3. What were the three most important things about King William's War?
4. Why was Queen Anne's War so short?
5. Why did the New Yorkers and the French make an agreement with each other?
6. What was the Albany Plan of Union?
7. Give two results of the Battle of Lake George.
8. Who was more successful during the first part of the French and Indian War, the French or the English? Give examples to prove your answer.
9. When did England begin to win?
10. What was the result of the French and Indian War?

THE WONDERFUL WORLD OF WORDS . . .
1. massacre	4. warriors	7. truce
2. historic	5. horror	8. temporary
3. murderous	6. determination	9. conquer

Chapter VII

CAUSES OF THE AMERICAN REVOLUTION

A Troubled Peace

CHAPTER VII

CAUSES OF THE AMERICAN REVOLUTION

THE FRENCH AND INDIAN WAR WAS OVER   Now, so everyone thought, life would be peaceful at last. However, trouble was in the air. There were two reasons for this. First of all, the wars with France had cost England a great deal of money. She needed to pay her war debts. The colonies were rich. So, England thought they should give the mother country the money she needed. Secondly, the Indians who had helped England win the wars were not happy. The white settlers were moving into their lands. They wanted England to do something about this.

England passed several laws during these years. The laws were passed in order to get money for England or to please the Indians. We shall discuss, very briefly, some of these laws.

THE PROCLAMATION OF 1763   A proclamation is an announcement. The English government announced in 1763 that no white settler would be allowed to settle west of the Appalachian Mountains. This made the Indians very happy, but it made the white people very angry. They had fought hard against the French in order to be able to settle on those rich lands in the Ohio Valley! They did not feel very kindly toward England after this law was passed.

The Proclamation of 1763 also said that anyone who wanted to trade with the Indians had to get a license, or permit, from the English government. You can imagine how the fur traders liked that law! They did not want any government to meddle with their business! The people who bought and sold land were unhappy with the Proclamation, too. They had planned to buy up the Indian land for a small price and then re-sell it to the settlers at a good profit. Now the Proclamation said settlers could not go west. As you can see, this law was not liked by anyone except the Indians.

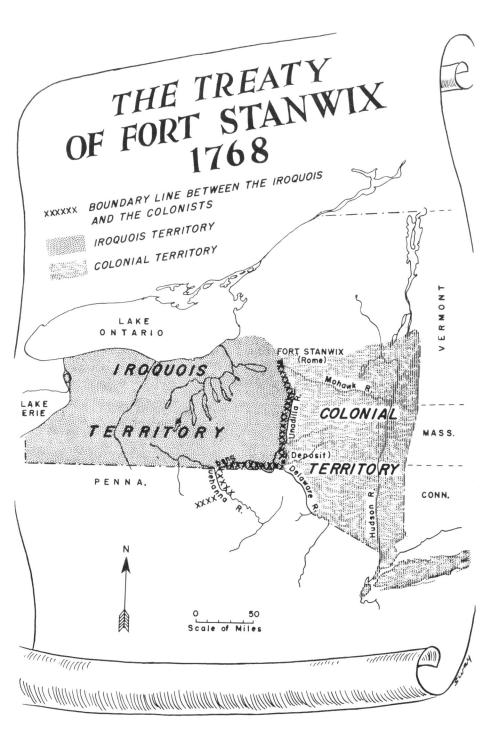

The Treaty of Fort Stanwix

In the long run, though, the Proclamation did not help the Indians very much. Many settlers refused to obey the Proclamation and settled in the west anyway. In New York the white people and the Iroquois made an agreement about the land. You have already read about it in Chapter II. This agreement was the Treaty of Fort Stanwix. It said that a line would be drawn from Fort Stanwix (Rome) to the Delaware River (near Deposit) and on into Pennsylvania. The white people said they would stay on the east side of this line. The Indians were to have all the land on the west side of the line. The white people of New York did not keep their promise. In just a few years many hundreds of them had crossed the line and made settlements on Indian land.

THE TRADE LAWS   The next thing England did which made New Yorkers and other colonists angry was to make rules about trade. England said that from 1764 on the traders must pay heavy taxes on the goods which they bought from the West Indies and other countries. The merchants said they could not pay the taxes and so the trade grew less and less. Many people were out of work. You can be sure that this did not make them like the English government.

THE STAMP ACT   In order to get money for the English government another law was passed in 1765. This was the famous Stamp Act. It said that a special tax stamp must be put on such things as newspapers, deeds to land, wills, contracts, college diplomas, and partnership agreements. The colonists hated this law. They said that only their own assemblies, elected by them, had the right to tax the colonists. They called the Stamp Act "taxation without representation." This means the tax was made without the approval of anyone from New York or the other colonies.

Many people refused to buy the stamps. When this did not get rid of the hated law, the colonists decided to refuse to buy any English goods at all. This is called a **boycott.** England could not stand to lose so much trade. The colonists then held a big meeting in New York City. It was called the Stamp Act Congress and it asked England to repeal, or take away, the Stamp Act. England agreed and the bad law was repealed. This made New Yorkers very happy and many of them quickly forgave England. After all, they were loyal Englishmen.

TOWNSHEND ACTS Two years after the repeal of the Stamp Act a new set of laws was passed in England. They were named the Townshend Acts after the man who was in charge of the English treasury. These laws put taxes on glass, lead, paper, paint, and tea. Again the New Yorkers were angry. Again they refused to buy English goods. In three years these laws, too, were repealed, except for a small tax on tea.

For the next few years New Yorkers lived in peace with England. There were no heavy taxes. Business was good. Trade was good. Trouble seemed to be over.

THE NEW YORK TEA PARTY Then the English government did something which the New York merchants did not like at all. It said that **only** the British East India Company could sell tea in the colonies. This would ruin the tea trade of the New Yorkers because the company could sell its tea cheaper. The merchants agreed to boycott anyone who bought tea from the company, that is, they would not buy from or sell to such a person. When the New Yorkers heard of the Boston Tea Party they decided they would do the same thing if a tea ship came into their harbor. The first ship did not even try to come into the harbor; it just turned around and went back again. When the second ship tried to land, New Yorkers did just as the "Indians" of Boston did. They climbed on the ship and threw all the tea into the ocean! New York had a tea party of its own!

THE INTOLERABLE ACTS To punish Boston for its "tea party" the English government passed laws called the Intolerable Acts. These laws closed the Boston harbor — no ship

Some causes of the American Revolution

could go in or come out. The laws also said that the Assembly could not meet. Self-government was taken away from the people of Massachusetts. New Yorkers were afraid that the same thing would happen to them. In fact, all the colonies were afraid. They were so worried that they held a meeting in Philadelphia to decide what to do. Every colony sent someone to the meeting except Georgia. This was called the First Continental Congress. The Congress decided on another boycott of English goods until the Intolerable Acts were repealed. New York thought this was too strong and did not vote for it.

THE WAR BEGINS   The next spring, on April 19, 1775, the first battle of the Revolution took place in the villages of Lexington and Concord in Massachusetts. When New Yorkers heard of it many got ready to defend their city and state. War for everyone was on the way. In May, Ethan Allen and Benedict Arnold with a small group of soldiers took Fort Ticonderoga away from the English. Not long after this, the English also lost the fort at Crown Point. The Revolutionary War had reached New York. It would remain for eight long years, years filled with bloodshed and sadness for thousands of people.

The colonies did not declare their independence right away. Many people did not want independence. They did not like unjust laws, but they also believed that the colonies should remain loyal to England. These people were called Loyalists. Sometimes they were also called Tories. There were a great many Loyalists in New York. Some were rich landowners, some were farmers and many were merchants. They were not bad people; they really believed it would be better for everyone if England went on ruling the colonies. When the Second Continental Congress adopted the Declaration of Independence on July 4, 1776, in Philadelphia, the New York men did not sign it. However, they did sign it five days later at a meeting of the New York government in White Plains.

THE WONDERFUL WORLD OF WORDS . . .

1. proclamation
2. boycott
3. Tories
4. taxation
5. representation
6. repeal
7. Congress
8. declaration
9. independence

TO HELP YOU REMEMBER . . .

1. What did the Proclamation of 1763 say?
2. Why were the merchants against the trade laws?
3. What was the Stamp Act?
4. Why did the colonists hate this law?
5. What did the colonists do about this law?
6. What did the Townshend Acts do?
7. What happened to the Townshend Acts?
8. Why did New York have a "tea party" in the harbor?
9. Who were the Tories?
10. When did New York sign the Declaration of Independence?

PERHAPS YOU WOULD LIKE TO . . .

1. Make a report on the Boston Tea Party and read it to your class.
2. Pretend you were a boy on the New York "tea party." Tell what happened.
3. Draw cartoons to show how the colonists felt about the trade laws and the Stamp Act.

Chapter VIII

THE REVOLUTION
IN NEW YORK STATE

CHAPTER VIII

1. New York City Falls to the British

In the years which followed the Declaration of Independence many important events took place in New York State. One third of all the fighting in the Revolutionary War took place in New York. In this chapter we shall read about some of those important events.

In the autumn of 1776 the English, under the leadership of General William Howe, captured New York City. Both sides wanted the city, of course, for many reasons. The English needed it badly in order to have a place for their ships to bring in supplies for the English soldiers. The battle for New York City lasted three months. From the beginning things did not look well for General George Washington. He had only 28,000 soldiers, while General Howe had 31,000. The English soldiers were well-trained and had good weapons with which to fight. They had been in wars before so they knew what to do. Washington's soldiers had very little training. Many of them were young and had never been to war before. Their supplies were poor; in fact many of them had only the muskets they brought with them from their homes. They put up a very brave fight but they were no match for the great English army.

One of the most exciting stories about the battle for New York City shows how calm and brave General Washington was. Some of the American troops were located at Brooklyn Heights. General Howe crossed over from Staten Island to Long Island and surprised the Americans. They were defeated, of course. When General Washington reached the battlefield he found his men so stunned by what had happened that they didn't know what to do. George Washington knew! That night, when everything was dark, he ordered his men to be **absolutely** still and to get into small boats. Rags were tied around the oars so that they would make no sound as the boats moved silently across the water of the East River to Manhattan. There, in the dark, while the English soldiers were asleep, General Washington saved what was left of his army! After that General Howe always called General Washington the Old Fox.

Washington's Headquarters at Newburgh

At the end of three months of fighting, New York City belonged to the English. It stayed in the hands of the English during the rest of the Revolution. The Americans lost many men during those three months. They also lost many cannon. However, they were not ready to give up.

2. Valcour Island

While General Howe was fighting for New York City, the English planned to have General Carleton come from Canada and capture the forts in northern New York. These were Ticonderoga and Crown Point. The American soldiers in the north had had a terrible winter. They had tried to take Quebec but had failed to do so. Many of the men had smallpox. They were a sad sight but they were not completely down.

Something had to be done to keep the English out of Lake Champlain. It was decided that under the leadership of their general, Benedict Arnold, they would build a fleet of ships. These ships would force General Carleton and his men back to Canada. As the work went on, the men's spirits rose, the smallpox grew less and the little "navy" began to grow. By September, sixteen boats were ready, with thirty-two guns.

Then Arnold sailed north with his fleet to meet General Carleton when he came down from Quebec. Carleton, of course, had found out about the plan, and had built himself a "navy" too—twenty-nine ships and fifty-three guns! It had taken him all summer to build the ships.

When Arnold heard that Carleton had started, he hid his own little fleet behind Valcour Island. When the English came in sight, he attacked. Twenty-nine is a big number compared to sixteen and fifty-three guns are better than thirty-two. Arnold and his brave little navy were defeated. However, they had done much good for the Americans. Because he had had to build his ships, Carleton had to put off an attack on Fort Ticonderoga. If he had been able to attack Ticonderoga in a good season of the year, and if he had won, the whole war might have turned out differently. In the Battle of Valcour Island, Benedict Arnold showed how smart and how brave he was.

3. A Turning Point

THE BATTLES OF SARATOGA AND ORISKANY

SARATOGA The most important battle of the Revolution took place in New York. This was the Battle of Saratoga in 1777. It happened because the English were trying to get control of New York. The English thought that if they could control all of New York State instead of just New York City, it would be impossible for the other parts of America to go on with the war. The supply lines would be broken and the colonies would not be able to get in touch with each other. To get control of New York, the English worked out a very good plan. This was the plan:

1. General Burgoyne (also called Gentleman Johnny) was to come south from Canada along the old "war-road" of the Indians: Lake Champlain, Lake George, and the Hudson River.

Neilson House, Saratoga Battlefield

2. General Barry St. Leger was to cross Lake Ontario, at Fort Oswego and continue through the Mohawk Valley.

3. General Sir William Howe was to come up the Hudson from New York City.

4. All three were to meet in Albany to celebrate their victory over New York!

It was a good plan, but it did not work out quite as the three generals thought it would. This is what happened. (This plan, like all other important campaigns of the Revolution in New York State, is also shown in your NEW YORK STATE ATLAS.)

Burgoyne took Fort Ticonderoga away from the Americans in July, 1777. He could do this because the Americans had not put any guns on Mt. Defiance, a small mountain which overlooks Ticonderoga. They thought no army could ever get up there. Burgoyne's army did! With enemy cannon up above, there was nothing the American general could do except try to get his men away safely. Most of the men found their way to Fort Edward.

There General Philip Schuyler thought of a way to slow down Burgoyne's march. He knew they could not defend Fort Edward but they could make things hard for Burgoyne. The road to Fort Edward was only a path in the forest with bogs and swamps on both sides. Schuyler had his men cut down the huge trees which grew there. They let the trees fall across the "road" and then turned the swamp water into the "road" to make it even nicer. The plan worked! Burgoyne had to work for three weeks in order to travel forty-five miles! In the meantime more troops came for the Americans and by August there were nearly 5,000 men in Schuyler's army.

Things began to look brighter for the Americans. Burgoyne lost many men when one of his German officers tried to get food supplies from the fort in Bennington, Vermont. John Stark, Seth Warner and the riflemen of Bennington defeated them completely. This is known as the Battle of Bennington.

Some Indians in the Burgoyne company had murdered a girl named Jane McCrea. This caused the farmers of the country-side to join the American army in order to get even. General Horatio Gates was now in charge of the army. In August, too, good news came from the west.

Courtesy of the New York State Department of Commerce
General Herkimer at Oriskany

BATTLE OF ORISKANY

You remember that part of the English plan to capture New York said that General Barry St. Leger was to come from Fort Oswego, down the Mohawk Valley to Albany. General St. Leger started out as planned. He intended to take Fort Stanwix first. However, he ran into real trouble from the beginning. The two officers in charge of the fort would not surrender. The county militia, under the leadership of General Nicholas Herkimer, started toward the fort to try to help. St. Leger sent his soldiers and Indians to ambush them and destroy them. An ambush is a surprise attack. A bloody battle took place at Oriskany, but the result was one the English had not expected. The militiamen won the battle even though their leader, General Herkimer, was badly wounded. He refused to give in, in spite of his badly wounded leg. He had his men prop him up against a tree and he went on directing the battle. His wounds were so bad that he died two weeks later.

Back at Fort Stanwix things were not going well for the English either. The leader of the fort, Captain Willett, took 250 men out of the fort very quietly. They discovered that the English, who were working on a road close by, had left their tents unguarded. The Americans quickly took all the supplies and were back in the fort before the English found out what had happened. The Indians shook with rage because all their possessions had been taken. They said they would get even with the Americans.

Help was on the way for the Americans at Fort Stanwix. General Philip Schuyler had heard about Oriskany and the siege of Stanwix. Benedict Arnold, serving with Schuyler, volunteered to lead a troop of soldiers to rescue the fort. When the Indians heard that a very large number of Americans was coming, they decided to leave and simply walked off into the woods. They had had enough! When that happened, St. Leger knew that he must give up. He ordered his soldiers back to Fort Oswego. His part of the great plan had ended in dismal failure.

The third part of the plan never did work out. General Sir William Howe was supposed to come up the Hudson from New York City. He never did, and we do not know why. He went, instead to Philadelphia.

The campaign ended with two battles which we call the Battle of Saratoga. Remember that the British general, Burgoyne, was coming from the north. He crossed the Hudson on September 15 at the place where Schuylerville now stands. In those days it was called Saratoga.

On September 19 the British and the Americans fought a battle which the Americans won. This was at Bemis Heights about eight miles south of Schuylerville. After it was over, both sides drew back. They just faced each other for over two weeks.

Then on October 7 the two armies met once more and again the Americans won. General Horatio Gates was in charge of the American forces. However, Benedict Arnold played a great part in this heroic battle. Also, he was wounded in the leg he led the American soldiers on to victory. General Philip Schuyler, another brave New Yorker, had a part in the battle. After the battle was over, General Burgoyne's army was in very sad condition. They had very few supplies and many of them were wounded or sick. Burgoyne tried to get his men back to Canada but General John Stark, the hero of Bennington, stood in his way. General Burgoyne then did the only thing he could do—he surrendered to General Gates on October 17, 1777.

General Burgoyne did not understand why General Howe had not come up the Hudson to help him. General Sir Henry Clinton did try to help by coming up the Hudson and taking two forts, Clinton and Montgomery. Then he heard that Burgoyne had surrendered so he took his small army back to New York City. The English campaign to gain control of New York was over. Gentleman Johnny Burgoyne was the only English general to reach Albany and he was a prisoner of war in Philip Schuyler's house!

Courtesy of the New York State Department of Commerce
Monument to Arnold's Boot

95

IMPORTANCE OF SARATOGA

The Battle of Saratoga was the most important battle of the Revolution because it was the turning point of the war. Before this the Americans had lost many battles. It seemed impossible to defeat the great English army. The English held New York and Philadelphia, the two largest cities. After the victory at Saratoga things began to change. The rest of the army was inspired by what had happened at Saratoga and began to win battles. Most important of all, the French came into the war on the side of the Americans. Because of the courage and the skill shown at Saratoga, France thought that the Americans might be able to defeat her old enemy, England. Therefore, France decided to loan America money for supplies. She also sent her navy over to help fight the English. In addition, Frenchmen like the Marquis de Lafayette came over and offered to help General Washington in the war for independence and liberty.

General Burgoyne surrenders.

4. Birth of New York State — 1777

Other important events took place in New York in the year 1777. This was the year in which New York became, officially, New York **State.** You remember that New Yorkers signed the Declaration of Independence on July 9, 1776. A committee was then set up to decide what kind of government the new state should have. In March, 1777, the committee finished writing a constitution for the new state. A constitution is a written plan of government. A club may have one; States, and nations almost always have one. The first New York State constitution was written mostly by a man named John Jay who later became the first Chief Justice of the United States.

The first Constitution said some interesting things. Some of these were:

1. There was to be freedom of religion.
2. There was to be trial by jury.
3. The whole Declaration of Independence was included in the Constitution.
4. There was to be a Senate, an Assembly, and a Governor.
5. To vote for a senator or governor a **man** had to own property worth 100 pounds or more.
6. To vote for assemblymen a man had to own property worth at least twenty pounds, **or** pay rent of at least forty shillings per year.

George Clinton was elected governor of the new state. The first capitol was at Kingston. The first legislature (the Assembly and the Senate) met there in September, 1777. They had to leave in a hurry in October, however, because the English captured Kingston and burned it.

5. The Frontier Raids

To understand what happened in New York State during the next two years we must leave the Hudson Valley and go to the

97

frontier. The events of 1778 happened where there were no cities and towns and no strong, well-supplied forts. In frontier country there were only a few tiny settlements, many lonely, isolated farms, and here and there a small stockade type of fort. It was here, on the lonely frontier, that the English and the Indians made many cruel raids during 1778.

The leaders of these raids were usually Joseph Brant, a great Mohawk chief, or Captain Walter Butler, a loyalist or Tory. Behind the scenes were three other men, Sir Guy Johnson, Sir John Johnson, and John Butler, Walter's father. These three men were tories who would do anything in order to win the war for England. They were the ones who planned the Indian raids. From May to November in 1778 the Loyalists and Indians burned at least one frontier settlement each month.

The worst raid of all came on November 11 when, in the dim, cold hours just before daylight, a yelling, screaming mob of Indians and tories, seven hundred strong, swooped down on the sleeping village of Cherry Valley. This time the Indians, led by Walter Butler and Joseph Brant, got completely out of control and were far more savage than they had ever been before. They killed and scalped men, women and children. Most of the buildings were burned and all the food supplies and animals were taken away. The Indians also took almost one hundred prisoners. However, after everything had calmed down, Brant let half of the prisoners go free.

REVEREND SAMUEL DUNLOP   During the Cherry Valley massacre, one man's life was spared through a strange circumstance. This man was the Reverend Samuel Dunlop. His wife had been killed during the raid that dreadful morning. An Indian, his scalping knife raised and ready to do its terrible work, stood over the Reverend Dunlop. The Indian grasped the preacher's hair, but the hair lifted from Reverend Dunlop's head, within the Indian's grasp. The reason, of course, was that the Reverend Dunlop wore a wig!

The Rev. Samuel Dunlop loses his wig but saves his life.

While the Indian stood and stared at the odd-looking "scalp" in his hand, an Indian chief appeared in the doorway. He saw what was going on, and stopped it. That is how the Reverend Dunlop's scalp was saved by his hair!

6. The Sullivan-Clinton Campaign

The Cherry Valley Massacre is very important in the story of the Iroquois Indians and in the story of the American Revolution in New York State. Because it was so wild and so savage everyone agreed that General Washington must do something to see that the Indian raids on the frontier stopped. The result was the famous Sullivan-Clinton Campaign which took place in 1779. The name comes from the two generals, James Clinton and John Sullivan, who led the campaign. The main idea of the campaign was to crush the Iroquois so completely that they could never again hurt a frontier settlement. (The story of the frontier war and the Sullivan Campaign is mapped for you on page 32 of your NEW YORK STATE ATLAS. It also shows the Indian villages destroyed and the white villages attacked or destroyed.)

THE BATTLE OF NEWTOWN   General Clinton started from Canajoharie on the Mohawk and marched south, burning deserted Indian villages on his way. General Sullivan started from Pennsylvania and marched his soldiers north. He also burned Indian villages and crops along the way. The two armies met at Tioga and together they marched westward and northward toward the country of the Genesee. They met very few Indians until they reached a place called Newtown near the modern city of Elmira.

Here there was a battle between the Indians and the white men. At the close of the battle, the Indians disappeared into the forest and the American soldiers went on their way. Their orders were to burn and destroy everything which belonged to the Indian. They burned village after village and field after field of Indian crops. No orchard was left, no sign of anything to eat. When the campaign was over, western New York was a sad place to look upon. The smoke rising from the burned villages and fields meant that thousands of people would be homeless and hungry during the coming winter. The Iroquois never got over the suffering caused by the Sullivan-Clinton Campaign.

7. Two Important Events of 1779

GENERAL WAYNE CAPTURES STONY POINT   One of the bravest, most skillful and most daring attacks of the Revolution took place in New York in July, 1779. This was General Anthony Wayne's capture of Stony Point on the Hudson River. The English had a fort there which they thought was so strong that no one could ever take it. However, General Wayne with a picked group of very brave American soldiers attacked the fort at night and captured it. Their plan was so daring and the soldiers were so skillful that the English were completely surprised.

BENEDICT ARNOLD BETRAYS HIS COUNTRY   The summer of 1779 is important for still another reason. That is the time when Benedict Arnold became a traitor. Arnold was in charge of the American fort at West Point. He agreed to surrender the fort to General Sir Henry Clinton. Why he did this we do not know. West Point was saved when American soldiers captured Major John Andre, an English officer who carried letters back and forth between Arnold and Clinton. Andre was hanged as a spy. Arnold went to join the English. This was an important event because if Clinton had captured West Point he might have been able to capture all of New York. However, it did not happen. After this New York State was never in danger again during this war.

THE LAST BATTLE OF THE REVOLUTION

The last battle of the Revolution took place in New York State at a place near Johnstown after the English had surrendered in Virginia. There a band of six hundred Indians and Loyalists was attacked by a band of Americans. The Americans won the battle and the enemy was forced back across Canada Creek. In this battle the famous Tory, Walter Butler, was shot through the head. It is said that he died face down in Canada Creek.

The fighting came to an end in 1781 but the peace treaty was not signed until 1783. Then the English finally left New York City. The American flag flew over the city at last. After eight years of dreadful war, New Yorkers and other Americans were truly independent and free to begin the building of a new nation.

8. Summary

The American Revolution took place between the years 1775 and 1783. In this war, the thirteen colonies gained their independence from England and became the United States of America. Because of its geographical location, New York State played a very important part in the Revolution. One third of all the battles of the Revolution were fought on New York soil. The most important battle was the Battle of Saratoga which prevented the English from capturing the state of New York. When the Americans won this battle, the French decided to give them help. This help was important to the

Americans in winning the war. Other exciting events which occurred in New York State were the capture of Ticonderoga, the Battle of Valcour Island, the Battle of Oriskany, the Indian frontier raids, the Sullivan-Clinton Campaign and the capture of Stony Point. The fighting ended in 1781 and the peace treaty was signed two years later.

New York suffered a great deal in the Revolution. Bloody fighting took place in every settled part of the state. Property was burned, innocent people were killed. Many people in New York State were loyalists or tories who wanted America to remain part of England. Feeling was very bitter between these people and the patriots. Many loyalists had to leave America

Breaking the dam at Cooperstown

and go to England or Canada to live. When the war was over, many people were poor and had to start their lives over again. There was much re-building to do. The people planted new crops and built new houses and villages. They spread out and settled in new places. They raised new families and made new friends. They started to build a new nation, free and completely independent.

WHEN THINGS HAPPENED

Battle of Lexington and Concord............April 19, 1775
Capture of Ticonderoga ....May, 1775
Capture of Crown Point 1775
Declaration of Independence
    Philadelphia ....July 4, 1776
    White Plains, New York...................July 9, 1776
New York City captured by the English................1776
Battle of Valcour Island ....Sept., 1776
Battle of Oriskany ....Aug., 1777
Battle of Saratoga ....Oct., 1777
First Constitution of New York State...........March, 1777
First Government of New York State.............Sept., 1777
Frontier raids...............................May-Nov., 1778
Clinton-Sullivan Campaign............................1779
Benedict Arnold's treason...........................1779
Battle of Stony Point...............................1779
Last Battle of Revolution...................Oct. 25, 1781

TO HELP YOU REMEMBER . . .

1. Which side held New York City all during the war?
2. Why is the Battle of Valcour Island important?
3. Describe the British plan to cut the colonies in two.
4. How was Burgoyne able to capture Fort Ticonderoga?
5. How did General Schuyler make things hard for Burgoyne?
6. What happened at Oriskany?
7. Why is Saratoga called the "turning point of the war"?
8. Why is John Jay famous?
9. What rights were included in New York's first constitution?

10. What was the purpose of the Sullivan-Clinton campaign?
11. Why was Benedict Arnold's treason so important?
12. When did the Revolutionary War end? Give two dates.

THE WONDERFUL WORLD OF WORDS ...

1. stunned
2. constitution
3. treason
4. traitor
5. treaty
6. campaign
7. frontier

VERY IMPORTANT PERSONS

ENGLISH
General Burgoyne
General St. Leger
General William Howe
General Henry Clinton

LOYALISTS
John Johnson
Guy Johnson
John Butler
Walter Butler
Joseph Brant

AMERICANS
George Washington
Benedict Arnold
Philip Schuyler
Horatio Gates
Nicholas Herkimer
James Clinton
John Sullivan
Anthony Wayne
John Stark
Marinus Willett
George Clinton
John Jay

PERHAPS YOU WOULD LIKE TO ...

1. Look up the route of General Washington's retreat from Brooklyn Heights in your New York State Atlas. Make your own map, using the big one as a guide.
2. Study the map on page 32 of your New York State Atlas. Make your own map of the Sullivan-Clinton campaign, using your own symbols.
3. Make a time line of the important events in this chapter. Your teacher will show you how.
4. Write a report on one or more of the VIP's who are listed at the end of this chapter.
5. Draw a map showing the English plan to cut the colonies in two. Your New York State Atlas will help you.

Chapter IX

ECONOMIC GROWTH AFTER THE REVOLUTION

CHAPTER IX

1. Land Claims Settled

Today most of the people in New York State live in cities. At the close of the Revolutionary War in 1783, just the opposite was true. In 1790, for example, New York City had only 33,000 people and Albany had only 3,500! In general, people lived in small settlements which contained ten to fifty houses. These settlements were located along the few dirt roads which were then in existence. Most of them, too, were located in the southeast corner of the state or close to the Hudson and Mohawk Rivers.

There are several reasons for this. Almost everyone entered the state at New York City and it was natural for immigrants to stay and make a living where their friends and relatives were already settled. It was also easier to make a living in the fertile land along the rivers and on Long Island. In addition to these reasons much of the interior of the state had been closed off to white men because of treaties with the Indians. You will remember reading earlier about the Fort Stanwix Treaty of 1768. It was not safe for settlers to go to the frontier to settle as long as there was an Indian problem.

After the Revolution the Indians realized that they could not keep the white men from living on their lands. One by one, the tribes sold their hunting grounds to the white man. By 1800 all their land was gone and the Indians were living on a few reservations.

Another thing which prevented western settlement was that no one was really sure who owned the western land. New York said she did; Massachusetts said she did. Massachusetts based her claim on her charter which had been issued by the King of England many years before. The charter gave Massachusetts the land from "sea-to-sea." New York, of course, hotly denied that Massachusetts had any right to the western lands. The quarrel went on until 1786 when a meeting was held at Hartford, Connecticut, to see if the whole problem could be settled.

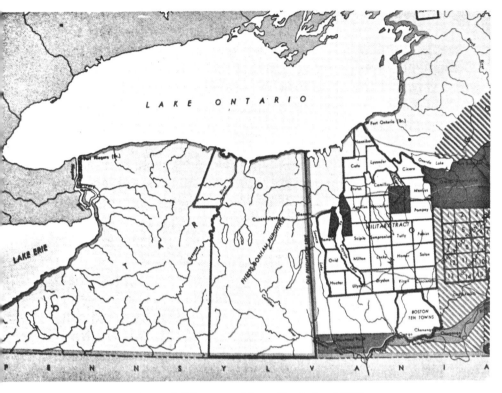

Map of Western New York in 1790

THE PRE-EMPTION LINE Here is how the state settled the problem. A line (called the Pre-emption Line) was drawn south from Sodus Bay through Seneca Lake to the Pennsylvania border. All the lands west of the line would belong to Massachusetts. New York would have all the lands east of the line. In addition, New York would have political power over **all** the western land. In other words, Massachusetts could sell the land and keep the money. The people who bought the land would become citizens of New York State. In this way, Massachusetts received all the money from the

107

sale of the land. New York received the land to settle and to tax thereafter.

In 1786 the state legislature named a group of men to be land commissioners. These men had the power to sell the public lands in central and northern New York. Public land is land owned by the government. For the next few years these men were very busy. They divided the land into townships of about 64,000 acres. They set aside lots for schools. The rest of the land was then sold to settlers or to land speculators.

THE MILITARY TRACT One large piece of land in this area was set aside by the state for a special purpose. This was the Military Tract which the government set aside for veterans of the Revolutionary War. It was a way that the state took to repay the soldiers. The tract contained one and one-half million acres. It was divided into twenty-eight townships, each six miles square. Each New York Revolutionary War veteran was given a plot of 600 acres. Officers received more, depending upon their rank. Not many soldiers settled on their plots, however. Many accepted the land and then sold it to a land speculator for hard cash. A speculator was a person who bought a large tract of land. Then he sold parts of it to many people, making a profit each time.

MASSACHUSETTS SELLS HER NEW YORK STATE LANDS You will remember that the New York State land commissioners could sell only the land in central and northern New York. Western New York land was sold by Massachusetts. First Massachusetts sold land to two men, Mr. Phelps and Mr. Gorham. They dreamed of making a fortune selling it in smaller plots to settlers. Things didn't turn out as well as they planned, however, so they turned back two thirds of the purchase. The next man to buy the western New York lands was Robert Morris from Pennsylvania. He, in turn, sold the land to several other groups, the chief one of which was a Dutch company called the Holland Land Company. The Holland Land Company, with its wise land agent, Joseph Ellicott, stayed in business for a long time.

MIGRATION TO THE WEST
All of these things — the land commissioners, the land companies, the land agents — helped settlers to move away from the crowded eastern part of the state. The direction in which people moved was almost always west. Some stopped their wagons in beautiful central New York. Others pushed on, taking their families and their treasures to the wild lands of the Genesee and beyond.

This migration of New Yorkers to the western part of their state was only the beginning of a much greater migration to the west of the United States. From travelers, people on the east coast heard tales of fine, fertile land, of forests filled with timber and animals, of rivers and streams to live by, all to the West. Many people wanted to see these wonderful things for themselves. So began the migration to the west. New York played an important part in this great movement. Because of her geographical location and because of the Mohawk River Valley, New Englanders who wanted to go west crossed New York State. The Mohawk River Valley provided the only northern pass through the Appalachian Mountains. From the western edge of New York it was not hard to reach the Ohio Country by following the shore of Lake Erie. In the years following the Revolution, New York not only settled her own western lands, she also became "the gateway to the West."

2. The Turnpikes

New York State did not really begin to grow until after some efforts had been made to give people cheap and good transportation. Settlers needed good ways to get to the west. The farmers on the frontier needed good ways to take their surplus crops to market to sell for cash.

The first main transportation routes used in New York were by water. There was the ocean for shipping and the good rivers and lakes for inland travel. However, there were some places where roads were needed. At first these roads were not much more than the old Indian trails. As more and more people used them the worse the roads became. Then the turnpikes were built. The state gave private companies permission to build and operate roads for profit. Such roads were called turnpikes. The state felt that more and better roads would bring more settlers into the state. More people meant that more trade and commerce would go on in the state. It all meant that New York would grow richer.

1 Pioneer Scene

THE FIRST TURNPIKE   The first turnpike, chartered by New York State in 1797, went from Albany to Schenectady, a distance of around fifteen miles. It cost $10,000 per mile to build this road, but when it was finished, it was the best road in the state.

MORE TURNPIKES   Albany was the turnpike center of the state. From Albany turnpikes went in all four directions. One important road went up the Mohawk Valley from Schenectady, another followed present Route 20 from Albany to the west. (RICHARDS ATLAS OF NEW YORK STATE has a large map which will show you the exact route of all of the turnpikes.)

By 1821 there were over 4,000 miles of turnpikes in New York State. However, after 1810 the private companies began to turn the roads back to the state. They could not afford to keep them up. One by one the turnpikes became just roads again. It is interesting that the first turnpike to open was the last to close. The road between Albany and Schenectady lasted until 1875 when it, too, stopped collecting tolls.

WHY TURNPIKES WERE IMPORTANT The turnpikes played a very important part in New York's growth. Because of the roads, settlers were able to settle away from the rivers and lakes. Crops were carried to market much faster and cheaper than before. Passenger travel was faster, too. It may not have been very easy to ride in a stagecoach but it was faster than an ox-drawn wagon! Because it was faster, people did travel. The people of one section learned to know what other parts of the state were like. This created a spirit of unity which is important in our development as the Empire State.

THE CLERMONT In August, 1807, an event occurred which was very important not only to New York but to the whole world as well. The **Clermont,** a steamboat built by Robert Fulton left New York City bound up the Hudson River for Albany. Thirty-two hours later, to the amazement of many, the puffing, chugging boat arrived safely at its destination. The return trip to New York City was made in 30 hours — 300 miles in sixty-two hours! No one had ever traveled so far so fast before! Those who had laughed at Robert Fulton, those who had called his boat "Fulton's Folly" now were glad to praise him.

Soon, many companies built steamboats and the rivers were crowded with boats of all sizes. Riding on steamboats could be very dangerous in those days. There were many

The Clermont

accidents because of swift currents or floating logs. Sometimes there were fires when sparks flew out of the smokestacks. This was especially true before they started using coal for fuel. Sometimes a whole ship exploded when a captain tied down the safety valve on his boiler in order to win a race with another boat.

STEAMBOAT TRAVEL IMPROVES In spite of these dangers, steamboats grew more and more popular. Of course they were improved each year and it became safer to travel on them. There was a regular service between New York City and Albany, another between New York City and the cities on Long Island Sound and still another between New York City and Boston.

The first steamship on the Great Lakes was the **Walk-in-the Water.** After the Erie Canal was built, Buffalo became a great steamship port. Immigrants came as far as Buffalo on canal boats, then were taken farther west by the steamships. On the return trip the ships brought lumber and wheat from the western frontier. This is one of the reasons Buffalo grew to be the imporant city it is today.

3. The Erie Canal

Steamboats were good, turnpikes were fine, but still the farmers in central, western and northern New York were not happy. They still needed a way to get their products to market which was fast and cheap. Some of the farmers had to take very long journeys to sell their goods and buy the things they needed. Montreal and Baltimore were the two chief ports, not New York City. The reason for this was that a farmer in western New York could get his wheat to the Genesee River, float it on rafts down to Lake Ontario and from there use the St. Lawrence River to take it to Montreal. Or, a farmer in middle New York could send his wheat, potash and lumber to Baltimore by using the Susquehanna River. Both ways were long and hard. Everyone wanted a better way.

"CLINTON'S DITCH" IS STARTED One man, DeWitt Clinton, governor of the state, did something about it. He thought that there should be a waterway all the way across the state. This waterway would carry freight and passengers safely, swiftly and cheaply from one side of the state to the other. DeWitt Clinton said that men could dig such a waterway. People laughed at him, called his idea "Clinton's Ditch" or the "Governor's Gully." They said that it never could be done. However, DeWitt Clinton refused to give up. He knew his idea would work. Finally, the New York legislature agreed with him. They voted to build the canal.

113

On July 4, 1817, at Rome, Governor Clinton turned the first spadeful of earth of the Grand Erie Canal.

The ceremony at Rome was the beginning of eight years of hard, back-breaking work in order to make a dream come true. What did it look like, this Grand Erie Canal? It was a ditch, dug by hand and sweat. It was 365 miles long, forty feet wide at the top and twenty-eight feet wide at the bottom. A tow path

Courtesy of the New York State Department of Commerce
Barge Canal, Lock 17 at Little Falls

was constructed at the side of the canal. Along this walked the "Hoggee" as he drove the patient mules or horses who pulled the boats along the canal.

A GREAT ENGINEERING FEAT Because of waterfalls and differences in elevation it was necessary to build sixty-five locks to raise the boats from one level to another. When the Erie found natural waterways or river gorges in its path, aqueducts were built to

114

carry the canal. An aqueduct is a bridge which carries water. At Rochester an aqueduct which had nine arches and was 802 feet long carried the Canal over the Genesee River. At some places, such as Little Falls and Lockport, the builders had to cut through solid rock.

The story of the building of the Erie Canal is a story of men who refused to be beaten. Much of the credit must go to the Irish immigrants who worked so hard. They endured great hardships in order that the Canal could be finished. Many of them died of malaria in the Montezuma Swamp before cold weather came to drive the mosquitoes away. Those who were left went on singing their cheerful songs. They worked all winter and had the Swamp section ready for boats in the spring!

The Grand Erie Canal was finished in 1825. To celebrate the great achievement, DeWitt Clinton and a group of officials rode in the **Seneca Chief** at the head of a procession of boats which traveled from Buffalo to New York City. At each town or city the boats stopped and there were great celebrations with speeches and fireworks. When the procession reached New York City, Governor Clinton emptied a keg of Lake Erie water into the Hudson River as a sign that the two were now joined. Then there were parades and banquets and more fireworks to celebrate the great accomplishment.

RESULTS OF THE ERIE CANAL The Erie Canal was indeed a great accomplishment for the state and for the nation. Let us list some of the things which happened as a result of the canal.

1. Farmers in western and central New York could send their products, such as wheat and lumber, to market cheaply. Freight rates dropped from $100 per ton to $10 per ton between Albany and Buffalo. The hauling time was cut from twenty days to eight days.

2. Products from the far west could reach the Atlantic much faster and cheaper than ever before.

3. Towns and cities grew. Some good examples are Rochester, Syracuse and Utica.

4. The "west" began to grow very fast. It was now easier to get to Illinois, Michigan, and Wisconsin. People traveled across New York State on the Erie Canal and then crossed the Great Lakes on steamboats.

5. New York City became the leader in eastern shipping. The Erie Canal started New York City on its way toward being the largest exporting and importing city in the world.

4. The Canal Era

OTHER CANALS ARE BUILT   The Erie Canal was so successful that other parts of the state also wanted to have canals. For the next few years New York State had a good case of "canal fever." Some of the smaller canals which were built during these years were:

(1) Chenango Canal which joined Utica and Binghamton on the Susquehanna River,

(2) the Oswego Canal which went from Syracuse to Oswego,

(3) Black River Canal which went from Rome to Carthage,

(4) Genesee Valley Canal which ran from Rochester to Olean on the Allegheny River.

This list is long enough to show that every part of the state wanted and got a canal during the years following 1825. However, very few of these canals were successful. Sometimes this was because they had not been really necessary in the first place. Sometimes it was because the railroad came along so soon after the canals. The railroads provided such strong competition that a small canal could not stay in business.

Barge Canal, near Fonda

In 1874 the people of New York voted that all the smaller canals should be closed except the Champlain, the Cayuga and Seneca, and the Oswego Canals. In 1882, the state made the canal toll-free. In the sixty-two years of its life up to that time, the Erie had paid for itself completely and left a profit of eight million dollars!

THE NEW YORK STATE BARGE CANAL SYSTEM

In 1903 the voters of the state agreed to spend over 100 million dollars to re-build the Erie, Oswego and Champlain Canals in order to make them good enough to carry modern commerce. Later more money was added and the Seneca and Cayuga Canal was included in the remodeling operation. The job was finished in 1918. The towpaths were gone, and there was no longer any need for the hard-working hoggee. Steam and diesel engines had taken the place of the plodding mule and horse. Wherever they could, the engineers moved the modern canal into the river beds and lake beds. Now they knew ways by which the level of natural waterways could be controlled. The "old Erie" was gone, but its descendant, the New York State Barge Canal System, lives on to serve the people of the Nation.

5. Railroads

RAILROADS ARE BUILT The first railroad in New York State was the Mohawk and Hudson which ran, as its name suggests, between Albany and Schenectady.

THE FIRST RAILROAD TRIP In August, 1831, the famous little engine, DeWitt Clinton, pulled its first train of three cars over the sixteen miles between Albany and Schenectady. The train didn't look much like our trains. It was a group of three cars which looked a great deal like stagecoaches whose wheels were made to roll along on wooden rails. Roll along they did while the tiny engine poured out a thick plume of black smoke! Cinders were in the air and in the eyes of the people who were brave enough to take the first trip. Sparks from the engine's wood-burner glowed in the air and caused the ladies' parasols to burst into flames. The men's tall hats sometimes looked like smoke-stacks. The coaches had no brakes. When the engine stopped, each coach did, too, suddenly, by bumping into the one in front! The story is that men riding on the train solved this problem by jumping off, pulling up fence posts, and jamming these between the coaches to lessen the jolts. The cows in the fields must have looked on in complete amazement and wondered what those crazy human beings were up to now!

THE RAILROAD AGE BEGINS It was an exciting trip and a historic one because it opened the railroad age in the whole nation. From that day on people were sure that this new way of travel was best. Every town wanted a railroad because each was sure that a railroad would make it grow larger and more prosperous. Many of the towns did get a railroad. In fact, in the early days of railroading, there were so many short lines that it was necessary to change trains at least three times between Albany and Buffalo. If you made all the right connections, if you and every train were always on time, the trip took only twenty-five hours! Of course, if you went from New York City to Buffalo, there were many more changes and many more hours. This did not last long, however, because New Yorkers saw that it was not

The DeWitt Clinton

practical. Before the Civil War, in 1851, the famous Erie Railroad was completed. This made it possible to go all the way from a point near New York City to Dunkirk on the west, a distance of 460 miles, without changing trains. Two years later, fifteen short lines joined together to make one big railroad line which ran from Troy and Albany on the east to Buffalo and Niagara Falls on the west. This was the first New York Central Railroad, the grandfather of the one we have today.

What effect did the railroads have on the Erie Canal? The men in the legislature were so afraid that the new railroad

119

would hurt canal business that they passed laws to protect the canal. A railroad which ran alongside, or near, the canal could not carry freight except in the winter when the canal was frozen over. You understand the reason for this law. The canal was owned by the state and the state collected all the tolls paid on the canal. The state thought it could not afford to let the railroads take business away from the canal. This law lasted until 1851 when it was repealed and railroads were allowed to carry any freight any time.

Traveling on trains before the Civil War was fast but it was not comfortable or clean. There were many accidents because of poor equipment. The road bed was rough and the passengers were jolted and bumped unmercifully. Soot was everywhere! Gradually, however, men began to find ways to improve railroad travel. They learned how to make better rails and roadbeds. Engines were made more powerful and the cars became

Courtesy of the New York State Department of Commerce
Leaving Lock 17 at Little Falls

stronger. George Westinghouse, a young man from Central Bridge, New York, invented the air brake, which made riding safer and more comfortable. The sleeping car, the parlor car and the dining car were invented by three other men from New York: George Pullman, Webster Wagner and Theodore Woodruff.

NEW YORK STATE'S TRANSPORTATION SYSTEM VITAL TO THE NEW NATION

Before the Civil War New York had built for its citizens a wonderful transportation system. This system consisted of ships, excellent turnpikes, the world-famous Erie Canal and a network of fast, dependable railroads. Because of these excellent means of transportation, freight rates were low. Goods could always be sent to market and cities grew and prospered. Good transportation helped New York become the Empire State. If you will think back to the days of the turnpike you will recall that the most important roads went from Albany to Buffalo, across the center of the state. The Canal also followed this route, you remember. The railroads, too, were built in this same region. The reason is, of course, because it is low land with no mountains to cross. This lowland route has been one of the chief reasons for the growth of New York State and also for the growth of the middle-western part of the United States. Goods, animals and people could be transported over the route with very little trouble. As transportation became faster, better and cheaper more and more people and goods went to the western part of the state and nation. The Irish who had built the Erie Canal stayed with it and helped the towns along its way to grow into big cities. People who built the railroads did the same. We can safely say that the new ways of transportation had a great deal to do with the settlement of New York State and the nation.

(If you will look at the manufacturing map in the RICHARDS ATLAS OF NEW YORK STATE, you will find this story repeated.) Again, most of the industries of the state are located along this lowland transportation route. Because the industries are there, cities are there and a large part of the state's population lives there. We cannot stress too much the importance of this lowland route across the state.

6. Manufacturing and Industry

WHY DID NEW YORK BECOME GREAT IN MANUFACTURING? In the years just before the Civil War, New York State became a great manufacturing state. What are some of the reasons for this? Let us list a few:

1. The excellent transportation system which we have just read about.

2. The location of New York City on the finest harbor in the country. This harbor made New York City the most natural place for all goods to come into the country and also for goods to leave the country. As a result, New York City very early became the trading center of the country. Raw materials entered there, were made into finished products in New York's factories and then shipped out to all parts of the world from New York City.

3. The city provided a good market for all kinds of things which could be made in other parts of the state.

4. There was always a large number of eager, willing and skilled workers. New York was the entering place for the millions of immigrants who came to America. All of these people wanted to work. Some of them were highly skilled craftsmen, others were not, but there was room in New York State's mills and factories for both kinds of workers.

New York possessed two more things which are necessary for a manufacturing state. She could get raw materials easily.

She had many streams to produce the power which the mills and factories needed.

CLOTHING INDUSTRY One of the first, and still one of the largest, industries in New York State was the making of clothing. Of course, New York did not grow cotton. But, because of its fine transportation system, this raw material could be brought from the South easily. New York did have the power with which to run the new spinning machines and looms.

LEATHER INDUSTRY Another early industry in New York was the leather industry. Not only did New York have the necessary animal hides from which to make the leather but she had another raw material as well. In those days the skins were tanned with a fluid made from the

Early tanning industry

bark of the hemlock tree. The Catskills, in particular, contained great numbers of these trees so that tanning became a big industry there.

IRON INDUSTRY Before the Civil War New York had a fine iron industry, most of it around Troy. Here is where the inventor Henry Burden lived and worked. The invention for which he is most famous is the machine which made a horseshoe every second.

SALT INDUSTRY The salt industry was another great industry in New York before the Civil War. There are great salt beds in the earth around Syracuse and salt from these beds went to all parts of the country.

LUMBER INDUSTRY Of course, one of New York's greatest natural resources is its forests. From these forests vast quantities of lumber were produced. Much lumber was needed for everywhere people were building homes, stores and factories. Saw mills were on almost every little stream and cities had much larger ones run by steam.

All of these goods just described are basic things. That means they are necessary. People cannot live without clothing and houses. As time went on, however, and people grew more used to machines and to buying products ready-made, the variety of goods increased. The market for manufactured goods grew and grew as people began to realize how much time and effort were saved by buying an article instead of making it.

7. Agriculture

LAND OWNERSHIP While great changes were going on in transportation, and cities and industries were growing up, things were also changing in agriculture. One of the most important changes had to do with land ownership. This change took place mostly in the Hudson Valley. In this region much of the land was owned by rich men who refused to sell land to the farmers who worked the land. Instead, the farmers could lease, or rent, the land from the owner. In return they had to pay a rent each year. This rent was goods and work and cash.

TROUBLE COMES This was not a good system and it did not work very well. The farmers did not like it because they thought that free Americans should be able to own the land they worked so hard. Many of the farmers refused to pay their rents.

Scene from the anti-rent wars

The landowners, of course, did not like this. They sent the sheriffs to the farms to collect the rents or put the farmer and his family off the land. This made the farmers even more angry. Real warfare started. The farmers put on calico dresses and painted their faces in Indian war paint. Dressed like this, they rode about the country scaring the landlords and their agents and the sheriffs, too.

These were called the "anti-rent" wars. Those were exciting days in the Hudson Valley. In Delaware County a sheriff was killed. However, all of this "fighting" did not change the laws. This method rarely ever does.

The farmers decided to try another more truly American way to get what they wanted. They began to elect men who agreed with them to the Assembly. Slowly things began to change. New laws made life harder for the landlords. They finally began to sell their land to the farmers. By the 1850's most of the big manors were gone and the farmers who worked the land owned it.

NEW AGRICULTURAL METHODS AND MACHINES

At about this same time farmers all over the state were beginning to wonder and ask questions about better ways of farming. They had never taken good care of their land. Now the soil was beginning to wear out. Agricultural societies were formed to teach more scientific ways of farming. In 1840 the state legislature decided to sponsor a state fair. Then the farmers and their families could see the best that was being done in agriculture in New York State. The first fair, held in 1841, was a great success. It became an exciting thing to go to the fair each year to see the fine exhibits of livestock, tools, fruits, vegetables and handiwork. The horse racing and sideshows were fun, too!

During the years before the Civil War several machines were invented to help farmers do their work. One of the most important of these inventions was the cast-iron plow invented by Jethro Wood in 1819. Other inventions which the New York State farmer was glad to have were rollers, corn planters and cultivators. After 1840 things began to look really bright for the farmer.

The farm in New York in those days was still the general family farm. The farmer grew many different crops and kept many kinds of livestock. He raised what his own family needed and as much more as he could. His surplus crops were generally sold to the nearest markets.

8. Population

One of the things which has made New York the Empire State is its very large population. Ever since the Revolution New York's population has grown larger and larger. Where did all these people come from and why did they come?

In the years following the Revolution people began to move into New York State from the nearby states of New England. Of course, some parts of New York, such as Long Island, had been settled by New Englanders many years before, in the 1600's. However, after the war, other New Englanders began to come. This time they came by the thousands, pouring into every city and town in New York State.

The turnpikes were a great aid to these travelers. They could use the New England roads as far as New York and then, when they had reached Greenbush or Hudson or Poughkeepsie they could go in any direction farther into New York. They came by sleigh and wagon and horseback; some probably even walked!

WHY DID NEW ENGLANDERS LEAVE? Why did the New Englanders want to leave their homes and come to New York to live? One reason was high taxes in New England states. Many farmers had lost their land because they could not pay the taxes. Another reason was the good land and the new, young, growing cities of New York. Soldiers who had been on the Clinton-Sullivan Expedition in 1779 took back glowing stories of the rich fertile land of New York State. It is said that an early pioneer sent back to New England his largest ear of corn in order to get his family to come on over to New York, too. Land agents sold the land at low prices and gave the pioneers a long time in which to pay. These are some of the reasons the early New Englanders came to New York.

Where did they go when they got here? The answer to that is — everywhere, except the Adirondack Mountains! In particular, the Yankees settled in the Hudson and Mohawk Valleys, in the area between Albany and Lake Champlain, in Schoharie Valley, in Otsego County and in the new cities of western New York.

127

So many Vermonters went to the region between the St. Lawrence and the Adirondacks that it was sometimes called "New Vermont." In fact, by 1850, one fifth of Vermont had moved over into New York State!

IMMIGRANTS HELP OUR SOCIETY These people from New England were very important in helping our state to grow. They cleared the wilderness and created new farm lands. They became leaders in trade and business, especially in the textile business. They were preachers, teachers, doctors and lawyers. Many were skilled craftsmen whose skills were necessary to our growing state. Our Yankee immigrants were such good businessmen that they made New York City the greatest harbor and port in the whole nation. They also made great fortunes for themselves. They brought with them many good ideas from New England. One of those was the idea that schools should be public, that is, paid for by tax money. We should always be grateful to these excellent neighbors who moved into our state and did so much to make it strong.

Courtesy of the New York State Department of Commerce
Statue of Liberty

NEW YORK HAS HAD MANY DIFFERENT PEOPLES COME

New York has had many other people move into it. The Irish came in great numbers in the 1840's. The Jews from Russia and central Europe, people from Poland, and people from Italy came after 1900. The Negroes came in the 1920's and the Puerto Ricans came by the thousands in the 1940's and 1950's.

There are many reasons for people leaving their homeland. We will learn more about these reasons when we study United States history. Here it is enough to say that America has always been a land of freedom and opportunity.

New York State has always had more immigrants than any other state. Let's see why this was so before the Civil War, then we will find that the same reasons were there after the Civil War. First of all, there were jobs. We were building canals and railroads. We needed help on our farms. We needed help to build houses and to work in factories.

Courtesy of the New York State Department of Commerce
This Canal came after the canal the immigrants helped to build.

New York also offered the newcomer some other things which were just as important as a job. Here he could worship God in whatever way he chose. Here he knew he would be able to vote as soon as he had done certain things. In those days this could not happen in Europe. Here the police would be present to help him and protect him. This was not always true in Europe.

All these things are reasons why so many people came to America from the older countries in Europe in the years before the Civil War. Many of the same reasons, as we have said, are true for the people who came after the Civil War.

This great flood of immigration affected New York State in several ways. First of all, it caused the cities to grow very rapidly. While some of the newcomers went to work on farms, the great majority lived in the cities. The cities grew so fast, in fact, that before the Civil War, almost half the people of New York lived in them. Secondly, the immigrants built the canals and railroads of the state as well as the millions of houses, stores and factories which were needed. They also provided a large working force to keep those factories busy.

Aqueduct crossing the Genesee River at Rochester

Many of the immigrants were skilled craftsmen and brought their skills with them to America. This was especially true of the Germans who settled upstate. Some of the immigrants even set up new industries. A good example of this is the Bausch & Lomb Company of Rochester which is famous for its fine lenses. This company was started by John Jacob Bausch, a German lensmaker who had come to seek his fortune in America. The Irish immigrants, especially, liked American politics and soon held great political power in the cities. They were almost always Democrats. Because of the Irish immigrants, the Roman Catholic Church also became a powerful force in New York State life. The Germans did not all belong to one church, but set up several different ones. Both groups brought with them their different customs and traditions. These have made life in New York State colorful and interesting.

Perhaps You Would Like to . . .

1. Take a trip on the Erie Canal. Keep a diary of all that you see and do, and share it with your class.

2. Pretend that you were on the DeWitt Clinton. Write a letter to a friend or a cousin telling of your thrilling experience.

3. Read the book "The Erie Canal" by Samuel Hopkins Adams. Make a report on what you read.

4. Have your teacher read to the whole class the canal stories in "Grandfather Stories" by Samuel Hopkins Adams.

5. Learn some of the songs the workmen sang as they built New York State. The canal songs are fun; so is Patsy-Ory Ory-Ay. They can be found in the Burl Ives Folk Song Book, or in the Fireside Book of Folk Songs.

6. Pretend you are the son or daughter of an immigrant family. Write a letter back to your old home telling what your new home is like.

To Help You Remember...

1. Where did most New Yorkers live when the Revolutionary War ended in 1783? Give two reasons why this was true.
2. How did New York and Massachusetts settle their quarrel over western land?
3. What was the Military Tract?
4. What was the difference betwen a land commissioner and a land speculator?
5. What was a turnpike? Where was the first turnpike in New York?
6. What part did turnpikes play in the growth of New York State?
7. Why is Robert Fulton famous?
8. Why was it necessary to build the Erie Canal?
9. Why was the Erie Canal so important to our state? To our nation?
10. How has the Erie Canal changed? What is the name of our canal system today?
11. Where was New York's first railroad built? Give a reason why.
12. What effect did the railroads have on the Erie Canal?
13. Why is the center of our state so important?
14. Give six reasons why New York became a great manufacturing state.
15. Name four of New York's chief industries before the Civil War.
16. How was the problem of land ownership finally solved?
17. What new inventions helped the farmer?
18. Why did so many people move into New York State before the Civil War?
19. Where did New York's new population come from?

The Wonderful World of Words...

1. speculator
2. migration
3. aqueduct
4. tow path
5. chartered
6. solution
7. tract
8. surplus
9. toll
10. population

Chapter X

POLITICAL ISSUES AND WARS FROM THE REVOLUTION TO 1865

CHAPTER X

1. Post Revolution Period

PROBLEMS OF THE NEW NATION After the war, people still had many problems. The new nation was called the United States of America. But no one felt united.

Each state made its own laws. It paid no attention to how any of these laws affected other Americans who did not live in that state. Some of the states used different money and would not accept money from another state. Some states put taxes on goods from another state. Things were very mixed up. During this time the only national government was the Congress of the Articles of Confederation. This Congress did little to solve the problems because it did not have very much power. Few people wanted the Congress to have power. They remembered how badly they had been treated when the English government had been strong.

However, the problems of money and trade became so great that the Articles of Confederation had to be changed. A convention was called to do this in 1787. The New York legislature agreed to send men to the convention: Instead of changing the Articles of Confederation, the convention wrote a completely new constitution. Remember that a constitution is a written plan of government. This Constitution gave the central government much more power than it had had before. Alexander Hamilton was the only New Yorker who would sign the new Constitution.

RATIFICATION OF THE CONSTITUTION Before the new Constitution could go into effect three-fourths of the states had to accept it. In New York State a great debate took place. One group wanted to accept, or ratify, the Constitution. They were called Federalists. Their leader was Alexander Hamilton. The people who did **not** want to ratify the Constitution were led by Governor George Clinton.

New York held a convention just for the purpose of accepting or not accepting the Constitution. All free men over twenty-one years of age voted for delegates to this convention. The convention was held at Poughkeepsie on June 17, 1788. On July 26 the Convention finally agreed to ratify' the Constitution if certain things were added to it. One of these things was a bill of rights. You remember that the approval of nine states was necessary in order for the new Constitution to go into effect. New Hampshire was the ninth state to ratify. Then came Virginia, and then came New York. New York could not live alone outside the union.

The first capital of the United States of America under the Constitution was New York City. There, at Federal Hall, on April 30, 1789, George Washington was inaugurated as first President of the United States.

John Jay house, Katonah, New York

TWO IMPORTANT EARLY NEW YORKERS

During the early days of our national history, New Yorkers were very important. Two men, in particular, will never be forgotten. They were Alexander Hamilton and John Jay. Hamilton was chosen by President Washington to be the first Secretary of the Treasury. It was Hamilton who found a successful way of paying the young country's war debts. It was Hamilton who got the Congress to set up a tariff as a way for the young country to get money. A tariff is a tax on goods coming into the country. It was Hamilton who set up the Bank of the United States. John Jay was chosen by President Washington to be the first Chief Justice of the United States. This meant that he was the leader of the Supreme Court. He was also chosen by the President to talk with England again in 1794 about problems the two countries were having with each other. The result of these talks is called the Jay Treaty. In this treaty England agreed to get out of the fur posts along the western frontier of the United States. In 1795 John Jay left the Supreme Court to become Governor of New York State. He was a very good governor for six years.

2. War of 1812

CAUSES OF THE WAR OF 1812

In June of 1812 the United States went to war again with England. This war, which lasted only a short while, is sometimes called "the second Revoluton." There were several reasons for this war.

(1) England and France were again at war with each other. The United States did not want to be on either side in the war. It also wanted to be free to trade with either side. The English navy would not allow this. In addition, they would stop American ships on the ocean, take the sailors off them and make them sail the English ships. Each time they would say they were taking only English sailors off the American ships! This is called "impressment" of sailors.

136

(2) A second cause of the War of 1812 was the way the Indians were acting on the western frontier. Many people believed that the English were telling the Indians what to do and helping them to frighten and kill western pioneers.

(3) A third cause of the War of 1812 was the wish of some Americans to conquer Canada and Florida and so make the United States much larger and richer.

NEW YORK STATE BATTLES OF THE WAR OF 1812

New Yorkers did fight in the War of 1812 and much of the fighting was done on the New York frontier. The hardship suffered by pioneer families in Western New York were very much like those suffered by

Mohawks on warpath in the War of 1812

137

settlers in the Mohawk Valley during the Revolutionary War. In the War of 1812, the British had the Mohawk Indians of Canada on their side. The Mohawks were fierce and cruel Indians, especially when they were full of whiskey. Their coming meant death and terror for everyone in their path. Night after night the settlers were wakened by a Mohawk war whoop.

The frightened white people fled from their beds as the Indians came swooping down on their tiny cabins. Into the winter night ran men, women and children, all trying to escape the awful tomahawks and the scalping knife. Many did not stop to dress. Shoes and stockings were forgotten. Feet were cut and frozen in the ice and snow. The homes which had taken so much hard work to build were left behind to be destroyed and burned by the war-mad Indians. The entire settlement at Lewiston was burned on December 19, 1813. So was much of the rest of Niagara County. Have your teacher tell you the story of the Gillette family of Lewiston. The story is in the book **Outpost of Empires.** Stories like this remind us that the War of 1812 was, indeed, an important part of our state's history.

In 1812 the English attacked Sacket's Harbor and Ogdensburg on Lake Ontario. The Americans drove them back each time. In 1813, the war did not go well for the Americans at all along the New York frontier. The English gained control of Lake Champlain. They also invaded the United States and captured Fort Niagara. The great American victory of that year was won by Captain Oliver Hazard Perry of the United States Navy. He crushed the English navy in a battle at Put-In Bay. This was important because it meant that Lake Erie was saved for the Americans.

In 1814 the Americans began to fight harder and better. They got control of Lake Ontario and then invaded Canada. There General Jacob Brown (from New York) won victories at Chippewa and at Lundy's Lane. The greatest victory of all, however, was at Lake Champlain. The English had control of the lake and planned to use it to invade the United States.

Their plan was much like the old Saratoga plan. The English general was to follow the path up the lake which Burgoyne had taken. Again the plan failed. The English had to face two men — General Alexander Macomb who was in charge at Plattsburgh, and Captain Thomas McDonough of the United States Navy. Captain McDonough defeated the English fleet and drove them out of the lake in the famous Battle of Lake Champlain. Without his ships the English general did not dare to invade New York, so he had to go back to Canada. This was the last important battle of the War of 1812 in New York State.

THE PRIVATEERS   Out of New York City the war was fought a little differently. In those days, during wartime, it was all right to put guns on regular ships.

Battle of Lake Champlain

These ships were then allowed to capture the ships of the enemy and bring home the cargoes. Such ships were called **privateers.** The ships they captured were called **prizes.** During the War of 1812, 120 privateers sailed out of New York harbor. They captured 275 prizes. This, of course, hurt England very badly.

NEW YORK CITY'S FRIGHT Only once was New York City really frightened by the war. This was in 1814 when the English attacked the new city of Washington, D. C. and set fire to all the new government buildings. New York City was afraid, then, that its turn would be next. Under the leadership of its mayor, DeWitt Clinton, the citizens built defenses and got ready to defend itself. However, the attack never came.

THE TREATY OF GHENT The War of 1812 ended in 1814 with the Treaty of Ghent. None of the problems was solved. No one really won the war. The best result was that England did have more respect for the United States as a nation.

3. First New Yorker in the White House

MARTIN VAN BUREN In 1836 a New Yorker moved into the White House for the first time. His name was Martin Van Buren. President Van Buren had been a powerful leader of the Democratic Party in New York for many years. In fact, he was so skillful in politics that his enemies called him such things as "Little Magician" and the "Red Fox of Kinderhook." Van Buren was elected governor of New York State in 1829 but he served only seventy-one days of his term. He left Albany to become Secretary of State for President Andrew Jackson. Then, in 1832, Van Buren was elected Vice-President of the United States, the second New Yorker to hold this high office. George Clinton had served earlier as Vice-President, from 1804 until 1812. In 1836, Andrew Jackson chose Martin Van Buren to succeed him as President

140

of the United States. Jackson's power was so great that Van Buren won both the nomination and the election easily. However, he did not have a happy time as President. In 1837 the country had some very bad times, many men were out of work and many banks failed. The people blamed President Van Buren and the Democratic Party for these things. Van Buren ran for re-election in 1840 but was badly defeated by General William Henry Harrison. In 1848, Van Buren again was a candidate for the presidency. This time he ran under the banner of the Free Soil Party about which you will read later. Again, he was defeated.

Martin Van Buren is still very much a part of our everyday lives. His home was at Kinderhook and many of his friends called him "Old Kinderhook." Van Buren had the habit of putting the initials of this nickname on anything of which he approved. Today we say a thing is O.K. when we approve of it or agree with it. A famous leader's nickname has thus become a part of our language.

4. The Slavery Issue Here

During the early years of our nation's history the people made great progress in learning how to live together happily and peacefully. New states were settled, new inventions made life easier, better transportation made it possible to know each other better. One thing, however, always divided the people of the north and south. That was, of course, the question of slavery. Was it right for one man to hold another as a slave? Many people, especially in the north, said that it was not right. Most people of the south said that it was not only right, but necessary as well. They could not run their huge cotton plantations without slavery. As more and more people went to settle the western territories the question became more and more important. The anti-slavery people did not want slavery in the new territories. Settlers from the south said they had the right to take their slaves with them wherever they went.

NEW YORK STATE FREES HER SLAVES

How did New York feel about the question of slavery? In 1799 the New York legislature passed a law which said that Negro children who were born after that date would be set free when they were grown up. In 1818 another law was passed which set July 4, 1827, as the official final date for slavery in New York State. There were very few slaves when that date came. Most Negroes in the state had been free for several years.

As the quarrel over slavery grew hotter and hotter, both of New York's political parties, the Whigs and the Democrats, were greatly concerned. Many people in both parties thought that slavery should be fought. Some people, of course, tried

New York State abolishes slavery July 4, 1827

to pretend that the problem did not exist. Other people grew angry enough to break away from the old parties and form new ones. The Free Soil Party which began in 1848 is a good example of this. The slogan of the new group was "Free soil, free speech, free labor, free men." As we have already read, this new party ran Martin Van Buren as its candidate for President in 1848.

MILLARD FILLMORE In the election of 1848 a New Yorker from Buffalo was a candidate for vice-president on the Whig ticket. His name was Millard Fillmore. In that election Zachary Taylor was elected President and Mr. Fillmore was elected Vice-President Soon after the election, President Taylor died. Mr. Fillmore then became President of the United States. While he was President he gave his consent to a very important law called the Compromise of 1850. This law was important because it settled the quarrel between the north and south for a little while. If the law had not been passed, perhaps the Civil War would have come in 1850 instead of 1860. President Fillmore, therefore, helped to put the war off for ten years.

THE REPUBLICAN PARTY IS BORN Another new political party was formed as a result of a law passed by Congress in 1854. This law, which was called the Kansas-Nebraska Act, said that the people living in the Kansas and Nebraska territories could decide the slavery question for themselves. This was almost the same as saying that slavery would be permitted. For thirty-four years before this time slavery had been definitely forbidden in these territories. When this law was passed, all the anti-slavery people in the North, both Whigs and Democrats, were very angry. They left their old parties and started a new one which they called the Republican Party. It is the same Republican party we know today. The new party said that it would do nothing about slavery in the older southern states. It would, however, fight to keep slavery out of the new territories of the west.

WILLIAM SEWARD   One of the most important men in the new Republican Party was a New Yorker named William H. Seward. Seward had been a Whig and a leading anti-slavery man for many years. When he was governor of New York State he refused to return runaway slaves to Virginia. When he was a member of the U. S. Senate he opposed slavery wherever he could. After Abraham Lincoln became President in 1860, he asked William H. Seward to be his Secretary of State.

THE ABOLITIONISTS   New York had other people, too, who were against slavery during the years when the Civil War was brewing. These people were called Abolitionists because they wanted to abolish, or get rid

The underground railroad

of, slavery. They worked in many ways. Some worked in anti-slavery societies. Some worked through their churches. Some, like Theodore Weld, went around making speeches against slavery. Others, like Gerrit Smith, spent great sums of money printing books and magazines to teach other people about the evil of slavery. Some helped slaves from the South escape to Canada where they would be free. This was exciting and dangerous work. White people caught in this act would have to pay a heavy fine **and** go to jail. The escape route was called an "Underground Railroad" because it was a secret transportation system. The houses or barns where the slaves were hidden were called "stations" and the brave people who planned it all and led the Negroes to freedom were called "conductors." Perhaps there is a house or barn in your community with a secret room which used to hide runaway slaves. Many a load of wheat on an Erie Canal barge hid a frightened Negro boy on his way to the North Star, the name which the slaves used for Canada. Many an ordinary New York farmer drawing his wagonload of corn to the mill sheltered a black face down under the golden ears. These were exciting days in New York State!

5. New York in the Civil War

ABRAHAM LINCOLN IS ELECTED PRESIDENT Abraham Lincoln was elected President of the United States in 1860. Not long afterward the southern states seceded, or withdrew from the United States. They started their own government which they called the Confederate States of America. In April, 1861, this government fired upon the United States flag at Fort Sumter, S. C. and the Civil War began. Let us see what part New York State played in this war. Let us see, also, how the war affected New York State.

From the beginning, New York sent men into the war. Boys and men rushed to enlist in the early months; in fact, by July of 1861 almost 50,000 had enlisted in the army or navy. At the Battle of Bull Run, the first battle of the war, one third of all those killed or wounded were from the Empire State.

145

The New York City draft riots

NEW YORK CITY DRAFT RIOTS

As the months went on, however, men were not quite so eager to go to war. At first the state tried to get more men to enlist by offering each a sum of money. Such money is called a **bounty.** Then the national government passed a draft law. This law said that all men between the ages of twenty and forty-five had to register for military service. Each state had to provide soldiers in proportion to its percentage of the total population. Since New York had the greatest population, it had to supply the greatest number of soldiers. This was not a good law and caused a great deal of trouble. In New York City the people rioted against the draft law. This means that they formed a huge mob which went about for three days burning the homes of abolitionists and doing other dreadful things. The New York Draft Riots were an ugly part of the Civil War.

NEW YORK STATE DOES ITS SHARE New York provided 464,701 soldiers for the Union Army. This was more than any other state. Of this number more than 50,000 died. This is a high percentage. The first northern officer to die in the war was Colonel Elmer Ellsworth of Mechanicville, leader of the colorful Zouaves. Forty Union Army generals came from New York State.

In addition to men, New York provided the greatest amount of supplies for the Union. Mills and factories were kept busy turning out cloth for uniforms, and blankets, shoes, guns, bullets. Every army has to eat and so the flour mills and the meat packing houses were kept busy, too. Jobs were easy to get and many men grew rich during the years of the Civil War.

You have all read, or seen on television, the story of the great battle between the Monitor and the Merrimac, the first ships to be covered with iron. The officer in charge of the Monitor in that historic battle was Lieutenant John Worden, a New Yorker. The iron plates which the Monitor wore were made in a factory at Troy, New York.

EFFECTS OF THE WAR ON NEW YORKERS As we have said, many kinds of businesses were helped by the Civil War. The canals and railroads, for instance, could hardly handle all their trade. Farmers were prosperous, too. The Army needed all their crops and was willing to pay well for them. New farm inventions made it possible for the farmers to increase their crops even though many of their sons were in the army.

Some industries, however, were badly hurt by the war. Cotton mills were forced to close because they could get no raw material. The merchant marine, that fleet of ships which carried goods from one part of the country to another and to all parts of the world, was almost ruined.

The Civil War had other effects on the lives of citizens which were not very pleasant. Taxes were very high because war, any war, costs a lot of money. New Yorkers paid more in taxes than the people of any other state. The poorer people suffered terribly during the war years because living costs rose so high. Prices were very high and wages were low. The wages which men and women made in the factories would not buy very much. This is called **inflation.** New York suffered greatly from inflation during the war.

People in small rural communities suffered from the war, too. Many of the young men went away to serve as soldiers and never came back. Many others went to the cities to work in the mills and factories and never returned to the farm or village.

New York State did, indeed, play a great part in the Civil War. It gave much to the Union cause in men, money and supplies. It also suffered much.

To Help You Remember . . .

1. How did New York feel about the new Constitution of the United States?

2. Where was the first capital of the United States located?

3. Why is Alexander Hamilton an important man in our country's history?

4. What did John Jay do for the United States?

5. In your own words, give three causes of the War of 1812.

6. Tell what these men did in the War of 1812: Oliver Hazard Perry, Jacob Brown. Thomas McDonough.

7. What was the result of the War of 1812?

8. Who was the first New Yorker to become President of the United States?

9. When did slavery officially end in New York? Why were most Negroes already free when that date came?

10. Who was Millard Fillmore? Why was he important?

11. Why was the Republican Party formed? How did the new party feel about slavery?

12. Who was William H. Seward?

13. What did abolitionists want to do? Tell three ways they worked to get what they wanted.

14. What was the Underground Railroad?

15. How did New York help in the Civil War?

16. How did the Civil War affect New York?

The Wonderful World of Words . . .

1. cooperation   4. inaugurate   7. privateer
2. solve   5. neutral   8. anti-slavery
3. constitution   6. militia   9. official

Perhaps You Would Like to . . .

1. Draw your own map of the War of 1812. Put on the map the important places mentioned in the chapter.

2. Write a report on Oliver Hazard Perry or Thomas McDonough.

3. Write a report on the life of one, or both, of the men who became President of the United States.

4. Pretend that your house was a station on the Underground Railroad. Write about your experiences in helping a slave to get to Canada.

5. Look up information about an interesting woman named Harriet Tubman. Tell the class what you find out.

6. Make an illustrated chart to show how the Civil War affected New York State.

7. Read more about the Monitor-Merrimac battle. Tell the class what you find out.

8. Draw cartoons to show how the people felt about the slavery question. You may use the slavery question in general, or such things as the Kansas-Nebraska Act or the beginning of the Republican Party.

9. Pretend that you were a Negro slave trying to escape. Write about your experiences on the Underground Railroad.

10. Draw cartoons showing how the people of New York felt in 1789 about the new constitution of the United States.

Chapter XI

NEW YORK GROWS IN CULTURE AND REFORM

151

CHAPTER XI

1. Famous New Yorkers in Literature

WASHINGTON IRVING We have seen how, in the years before the Civil War, New York State grew in wealth, in industry and in population. The state grew in still other ways. Many of its people became very skilled in such things as art, music, the theater and literature. We call these things the "cultural" parts of a state or nation. The first American to become really famous as a writer during these years was Washington Irving, the son of a successful New York merchant. Irving was a jolly man who liked to look at the funny side of life. He amused many people both in America and in Europe with his "Knickerbocker's History of New York." In this book Irving poked gentle fun at New York as it was when the Dutch were in control. Another famous book was Irving's "Sketch Book" which contained two stories you are sure to know, "Rip Van Winkle," and "The Legend of Sleepy Hollow." The people in these stories are a well-loved part of American folklore. The stories are about olden times on the banks of the Hudson and show us very clearly what life was like among the Dutch people in the Hudson Valley.

1. Washington Irving

2. James Fenimore Cooper

JAMES FENIMORE COOPER James Fenimore Cooper was the most famous American author of his day. His books, which were read all over Europe, were the first American books to use Indians as characters.

You know Cooper best for his famous "Leatherstocking Tales," the adventures of the famous and fearless Natty Bumppo and his Indian friends in the New York wilderness. James Fenimore Cooper was a great storyteller who wrote more than thirty thrilling stories of the wilderness and the sea.

WALT WHITMAN One of the greatest of all American writers was Walt Whitman. Whitman was born on Long Island, but grew up in Brooklyn. He didn't go to school very long but he did many other things. He was a carpenter, a typesetter, a newspaper reporter, a school teacher, an office boy, a traveler, a nurse during the Civil War, and a newspaper editor. However, Walt Whitman is best known as a poet. He wrote poetry about people and about America. He believed that people were good and that democratic America was the greatest place on earth. Because of his poems he has often been called the "poet of democracy." One of his most famous poems is "O Captain, My Captain" which he wrote after President Lincoln was killed.

1. Walt Whitman

2. Herman Melville

HERMAN MELVILLE Another famous writer who was a New Yorker was Herman Melville. Melville was an Albany boy who went to sea when he was young. He made two long voyages on whaling ships. Perhaps that is why he could write the great novel called "Moby Dick." This novel is about the adventures of Captain Ahab as he searched for the great white whale called Moby Dick. Perhaps you have seen the movie which was made from this book.

153

2. New York's Great Editors

BENJAMIN DAY AND THE NEW YORK SUN There were other men whose names are linked with writing in the first half of the nineteenth century. These men were great newspaper editors. In 1833 Benjamin Day started the New York Sun which was the first successful penny journal. In his paper Mr. Day printed all sorts of stories which he thought would interest his readers. People who could not afford to buy books could buy a penny journal.

JAMES GORDON BENNETT Day was so successful that James Gordon Bennett, editor of the New York Herald, decided he would do the same thing. In addition he used many pictures and gathered news quickly. The stories Bennett printed were not always good literature but they were interesting to people.

1. James Gordon Bennett

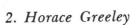

2. Horace Greeley

HORACE GREELEY AND CHARLES A. DANA The most famous editor of all was Horace Greeley who started the New York Tribune in 1841. Mr. Greeley was a crusader and published a crusading paper. This means that he wrote excellent articles in favor of such things as women's rights and public education. His editorials educated people about things which needed changing in their city and state. Horace Greeley is one of the greatest editors in our history. His managing editor, Charles A. Dana, was also a good writer.

1. *Charles Dana*

2. *Henry Raymond*

HENRY RAYMOND In 1851 Henry Raymond started the New York Times. This paper did not crusade. It printed stories of interest to the whole family. The Times printed the news, carefully, clearly, and honestly. Because of these great newspapers, New York became the leader in the newspaper field.

3. New York Leads the Way in Education

GEORGE CLINTON George Clinton, the first governor of New York State, knew that if the new state were to be a real democracy its citizens must be educated people. In colonial times, not even half the people of New York had gone to school. Therefore, Governor Clinton asked the legislature to set up the Board of Regents of the University of the State of New York. This group was given the right to set up schools and colleges.

DISTRICT SCHOOL LAW The first really important step in the growth of New York's great public school system was taken in 1812. The legislature passed the District School Law which gave the people of a village or neighborhood the right to choose three trustees, build a school, hire a teacher and collect taxes to help pay for it all. Each district also received a small amount of money from the state to help pay for the school. This did not mean that the district schools were free. They were not. State aid and taxes did not cover all the cost of the school, so each parent had to pay a certain sum for each of his children who attended the school. If the parent could not pay, his children could go to the school only if he signed a paper called a "pauper's oath." This paper said that the parent was too poor to pay and wished his children to go to school free. Many parents were too proud to sign such a paper and so their children never went to school.

GIDEON HAWLEY   The District School Law of 1812 also said there should be a state superintendent of schools. The man chosen to be the first state superintendent was Gideon Hawley, a Yankee who had moved to Ballston Spa in Saratoga County. Hawley held his post for many years and when he finally left it there were many district schools in New York State. They were known as the best schools in the nation.

PUBLIC SCHOOLS   Many people believed that schools should be completely free. DeWitt Clinton was one of these. He knew that it helps each of us if everyone is well educated. However, many others fought the idea of public schools. Some well-to-do people felt they should not have to pay for the education of their neighbors' children. Private schools were afraid public schools would ruin them. Church schools also did not like the idea of public schools. Even some parents did not want their children to go to school; they wanted them to go to work, instead. In 1867, however, the state legislature finally said that all public schools were to be free to all students.

In 1835 the legislature said that cities and large school districts could set up free high schools for those students who wanted to prepare for college. Before this time, if a boy wanted schooling beyond the district school he had to go to a private academy. This cost a great deal of money. Girls were sent to ladies' seminaries, which also charged tuition. (Tuition is money paid for education.) Under the new law of 1835 any boy or girl could go to high school for much less money. These schools were called Union Free Schools. Sometimes they took

156

Union College, Schenectady

over a private academy and even kept the name. An example of this is the Delaware Academy at Delhi. Perhaps you know of others.

Just before the Civil War there were fifteen colleges in New York State. One, the oldest, was in New York City. This was Columbia College which is now the great Columbia University. The other fourteen were upstate. The oldest of these was Union, founded in Schenectady in 1795. This college was a leader in education from the beginning. It was the first college anywhere to teach science by the laboratory method. It was also the first to allow boys to take French instead of Greek or Latin. It also allowed its students to choose some of the subjects they would take. Some of the other upstate colleges were West Point, for the training of military leaders; Rensselaer Polytechnic Institute at Troy for the training of engineers, and Hamilton, Colgate, Rochester, Hobart, St. Lawrence, and Alfred.

4. Fine Arts Grow in New York State

The outstanding artists, musicians and actors of the nation were from New York. One group, known in art history as the Hudson River School, painted many pictures of the beautiful Hudson Valley and the Catskill Mountains. The most famous of these painters were Frederick Church and Thomas Cole. William Sidney Mount, a Long Islander, painted wonderful pictures of people instead of scenery. In 1842 a group of musicians in New York City formed the Philharmonic Society of New York and began giving concerts. Today we call this group the New York Philharmonic Symphony Orchestra. It still gives concerts every week and thrills millions of people who listen to it on radio and television. Immigrants from Germany and Italy made New York City the leader in music in our country, a place which it still holds today.

Courtesy of the New York State Department of Commerce
Metropolitan Museum of Art

Today the theater capital of the country is Broadway in New York City. Every actor and every playwright hopes someday to be seen or known in New York City. This was true before the Civil War, too. The two plays seen most often were Uncle Tom's Cabin and Rip Van Winkle.

5. Aid to the Unfortunate

Before the Civil War there were a great many very poor people in New York State. There was no social security law in those days and no unemployment compensation. If a man had no job he had a hard time. Sometimes, of course, his family helped him out. If he had no family, or if they could not help him, the town tried to keep him from starving. Sometimes the town sold the services of the poor to some farmer who needed extra hands. The farmer paid the town and agreed to feed the workers. Many times, however, the poor worker got very little to eat. Finally, the state thought of a better plan. Each county would have a county poorhouse and the poorhouse would have a farm. The poor would work on the farm and so help pay for their keep at the poorhouse. This system lasted for a long time although it was never a good way of helping the poor. Our modern ways are much better.

Other people who were not treated well in earlier days were the insane people. It was not known in those days that insanity is an illness and needs the best doctors and hospitals. Then people thought that the insane persons were filled with devils. They kept them locked up in cages in the jails or poorhouses. There was no special hospital for these sick people until reformers demanded that the state build one. The first hospital for insane people was built at Utica.

A reformer is a person who wants to change things to make them better. There were many reformers in New York before the Civil War. They not only worked for better care for the insane, they tried to change the way criminals were treated, too. They succeeded in many ways. Whipping was stopped as a punishment. The number of crimes for which a person could be hanged was cut down. Young people were separated from older criminals.

Reformers were also busy during these years trying to get people in New York to stop drinking alcohol. So many men were drunkards in those days that homes and families were ruined. These reformers, who were called "temperance leaders" tried to do two things: (1) They tried to get people to sign a paper in which they promised never to drink again. (2) They tried to get the state of New York to forbid the selling of alcohol anywhere in the state.

Reformers also believed that prisons should help the criminals to become better people when they returned to the world outside. The first reformatory in the United States was the one in New York — the New York House of Refuge, set up in 1824.

The temperance movement did get many people to sign the pledge and so helped the problems caused by heavy drinking. The reformers did not succeed, however, in getting the state to forbid the sale of alcohol.

The Seneca Falls Convention

6. The Fight for Women's Rights

One of the most interesting parts of New York history is the story of the fight for women's rights. Perhaps this does not sound very exciting to you girls of today. If you had been a young woman a hundred years ago, you would have felt differently. Women have many rights now, then they had very few. For example, they could not go to college, or become a doctor or lawyer. They could not vote. They could not hold office. In fact, if a married woman earned money, her husband could take it all. If a girl's father left her property when he died, the property immediately went to the husband when the girl married. Even children were the father's property; he could take them away from the mother at any time, or will them to someone else! Things like these are what started the movement for women's rights.

ELIZABETH CADY STANTON AND SUSAN B. ANTHONY
The two great leaders in that fight were Elizabeth Cady Stanton and Susan B. Anthony. In 1848 Mrs. Stanton held a convention in Seneca Falls to which came women who wanted more rights. In 1850 the young school teacher, Miss Anthony, joined with Mrs. Stanton. These two women spent the rest of their lives fighting for what they knew was right. They were laughed at and insulted but they never gave up. In time many people began to respect them and agree with them. In 1872 Susan B. Anthony actually voted! Of course, she was arrested. The judge said she must pay a fine or go to jail. Miss Anthony refused to pay the fine and the judge never sent her to jail! Before the Civil War, the women made much progress in their fight. Finally the state legislature admitted they were partly right, at least. They passed a law which did two important things:

1. Women were given control of their property and the money they earned.

2. Women were made equal with their husbands in control of their children.

Women did not get the right to vote in state elections until 1917. However, they could vote in local elections before this. In 1919 women all over the United States were finally given the right to vote.

What about schooling? Were girls allowed to go to school? Schools just for girls began to appear in New York State. In 1821 Emma Willard started a school in Troy. Elmira College for Women opened in 1855. Elmira was the first college exclusively for women in the United States. Vassar College in Poughkeepsie opened in 1865. The first university to allow both men and women to attend was Cornell University.

ELIZABETH BLACKWELL Elizabeth Blackwell was a very brave girl. In days when no one else would do it, Elizabeth entered college at Geneva, determined to be a doctor. She was treated unkindly but she stayed right there and in 1849 she was graduated. Elizabeth Blackwell was the first woman doctor in the United States.

7. Help for the Working People

Life was not easy for the working people in the years before the Civil War. Most of them lived in slums in the big cities. Especially in New York City poverty was very bad. Most of the work in the factories and mills was done by women, children, and day laborers. In those days it was necessary for children to work, too, to help the family live. Children seven years old often worked from sunrise to sunset. The day laborers were often the immigrants who had just arrived in this country. They were not skilled craftsmen, but they would work hard at any job. These people all worked long hours for very low wages. It was even possible to put a man in jail because he owed a small debt. Many women in New York City did sewing in their own homes for the factory owners. They often had to work twelve or fifteen hours a day for about thirty cents. In 1855 a man who worked in a textile mill got about nineteen dollars per month.

UNIONS ARE FORMED   Of course things like this do not go on forever in a growing democracy. The working people wanted shorter hours, more pay, better working conditions and a chance for their children to go to school. They organized themselves into groups called **unions** to try to get these things from their employers and from the state. Little by little, they were successful. In the 1830's the legislature repealed the law which said a man could go to jail for a debt. Also, free public education grew and more and more of the workers' children could go to school. By 1860 most workers in most factories and mills were working only ten hours each day, six days each week.

To Help You Remember...

1. Name four New Yorkers who were famous in literature before the Civil War. What did each write?
2. What is an editor? Name four great editors of New York.
3. Why is George Clinton famous in the history of education?
4. What happened in education in 1812?
5. Tell what the District School Law said.
6. Give an important reason why many children did not go to school during these years.
7. Who was Gideon Hawley? Why was he important?
8. Give four of the arguments against public schools.
9. What was a Union Free School?
10. Name five colleges which New York had before the Civil War.
11. Who were the famous artists in New York before the Civil War? What did they paint?
12. What is a reformer?
13. Explain three things which the reformers of New York tried to do.
14. Who was Susan B. Anthony?
15. When did women get the right to vote in New York State? in the United States?

Wonderful World of Words ...

1. editor
2. reformer
3. temperance
4. unions
5. reformatory
6. academy
7. trustee

Perhaps You Would Like to ...

1. Read one of Washington Irving's books and make an illustrated report of it.

2. Draw posters to advertise the books by Washington Irving, James Fenimore Cooper, and Herman Melville.

3. Read one of James Fenimore Cooper's books and make a report on it to your class.

4. Learn all, or parts, of the poem "Oh Captain, My Captain."

5. Prepare a class newspaper called the Penny Journal so that you can learn about the problems of an editor. Include in your paper all the junior high school news and essays and articles written by class members.

6. Write a letter to the editor in which you give the arguments against public schools.

7. Look up more information about Elizabeth Cady Stanton, Susan B. Anthony, and Elizabeth Blackwell. Write a report and read it to your classmates.

8. Prepare a "What's My Line" program for your class. Use the people mentioned in this chapter.

Chapter XII

NEW YORK BECOMES THE EMPIRE STATE

1. Changes in Agriculture
2. Growth of Industry
3. Changes in Labor
4. Changes in Transportation

CHAPTER XII

NEW YORK BECOMES THE EMPIRE STATE

In the one hundred years which have gone by since the time of the Civil War, the economic life of New York State has changed completely. Let us look at four different parts of our state's economic life and see how each has changed since 1865. We will discuss agriculture, industry, labor, and transportation, the four things which make New York State the richest state in the nation.

1. Changes in Agriculture

AGRICULTURE Before the Civil War more than half of all New Yorkers lived on farms. That is not true today. Today only one out of twenty farm for a living. Farming today is done with machines instead of men. Farmers started finding substitutes for manpower when many young men did not come back from the Civil War. For many years they used horsepower instead of manpower. Then the gasoline engine was invented and the farmer discovered a whole new way to farm. One man on a tractor could do the work of many men and horses. A farmer with a truck could get his products to market in half the time it used to take.

In the years following the Civil War farmers started learning better ways of farming. These ways improved both the amount and the quality of their products. In 1865 the agricultural college at Cornell University was set up by the state. In later years the state set up two-year agricultural schools in Morrisville, Delhi, Cobleskill and Potsdam. The first agricultural experiment station in our country was set up by Congress at Geneva, New York. The purpose of this station was to develop new crops and study better ways of growing crops. In each county, as many of you know, there is a man who represents the Department of Agriculture. He is called a "county agent" and his job is to help the farmers in his county do a more scientific job of farming.

In the last one hundred years New York State has become chiefly a dairy state. In 1950, for example, half of the farm income came from the dairy industry.

2. Growth of Industry

INDUSTRY For more than a hundred years New York has led all the other states in industry. Since the Civil War, industry in New York has grown steadily both in the number of industries and the size of industries.

NEW LOCATIONS OF INDUSTRY In earlier days most factories were located in the largest cities. During recent years more and more companies have built new plants on the edges of the cities, sometimes even in the rural areas.* These new plants are often small, very attractive places.

*Electronics Park is located alongside the New York State Thruway—about seven miles northwest of Syracuse, near Liverpool, New York. There are sixteen buildings, more than five miles of paved roads, 5½ miles of railroad tracks, and 22 parking lots which can accommodate 5,900 employee cars.

Courtesy of the General Electric Corporation
New York State industry moves to the suburbs.

3. Changes in Labor

Perhaps the greatest changes of all have come in the field of labor. As the Industrial Revolution spread, fewer and fewer things were made by hand. The machine took over. Millions of people were needed to run the machines and most of them required little real skill to run them. In fact, many machines were run by untrained women and children.

LABOR UNIONS As the number of workers in the factories grew, so did the problems. To try to solve some of these problems labor unions began to grow. A labor union is an organization of workers. Its main purpose is to solve the problems of the workers by working on them together. What were some of the problems the early unions tried to solve? One, of course, was that of long hours. We have already read of the long hours which workers of an earlier day endured. Another problem was low wages and another was unsafe working conditions.

THE FIRST STRONG LABOR LAW One of the best ways to solve the problems of the working men and women is to have the legislature pass laws. In New York State the legislature has passed many laws to protect workers. The first strong labor law was passed in 1886. This law said that no child under thirteen could work in factories. It also said that no person under twenty-one could work more than sixty hours per week. The law also said that a factory inspector would enforce this law.

COMPENSATION There was a terrible fire in New York City in 1910 called the Triangle Shirtwaist fire. Many young women workers were burned to death. One of the results of that fire was a law which did two things. The law set up standards of safety which all factories had to follow. Second, the law said that if a worker was hurt while working, or if he became ill because of his job, the employer had to pay him part of his wages and also pay his medical bills. We call this "workmen's compensation." All workers have this compensation today.

UNEMPLOYMENT INSURANCE In 1930, during the great business depression, New York passed a law which gave help to old people. Later, in 1935, the Social Security program was passed by Congress. This law asked states to set up unemployment insurance plans. When a worker is out of work, he receives money from the state until he can find a job.

QUINN-IVES LAW One of the most important labor laws passed by the New York State legislature was the Quinn-Ives Law, passed in 1945. Because of this law, a person cannot be denied a job just because of his race or religion.

You can see from this brief description that New York State has been a leader in improving working conditions.

4. Changes in Transportation

New York's great transportation system has also grown and changed in many ways since the Civil War. We have already read how the Erie Canal was changed and improved until it finally became the Barge Canal System of today.

EARLY GROWTH OF THE RAILROADS Railroad transportation also grew by leaps and bounds after the Civil War. In 1860 New York had 2,682 miles of railroad track. In just forty years, that is, by 1900, there were 8,100 miles of track in the state. Railroads appeared in every section of the state.

Towns begged them to come. In some cases, people were willing to pay the railroad builders money if they would only build through their town. They hoped to grow into prosperous cities because of the railroad. Sometimes this happened, other times it did not.

FOUR MORE RAILROAD LINES ARE BUILT

The western part of the state was served by two railroads which came up from Pennsylvania and went to Buffalo. These were the Delaware, Lackawanna and Western and the Lehigh. Another important railroad was the Delaware and Hudson which ran from Binghamton on the southern border, through Albany, to Montreal on the north. This railroad helped the towns in the Lake Champlain Valley and the St. Lawrence Valley. (If you will look at the railroad map in your Richards Atlas you will also see railroad lines going through the western Adirondacks.) The cities of Watertown and Ogdensburg were helped to grow by a branch which the New York Central built between Utica and Montreal.

THE LONG ISLAND RAILROAD

Another important railroad which we must not forget is the famous Long Island Railroad. Each day thousands of people ride this railroad from Long Island to their work in the heart of New York City.

Courtesy of the New York State Department of Commerce

A modern industrial plant at Engineer's Hill Industrial Park Plainview, Long Island

170

In spite of many improvements made in railroads during the last fifty years, it is a fact that there are fewer miles of railroad track now than there were in 1900. Many small lines have been done away with. Many small stations have been closed. Some railroads, such as the New York, Ontario and Western, have gone out of business completely. One of the main reasons for this decline in railroad business is the great growth in transportation by automobile and airplane.

THE AUTOMOBILE AND BAD ROADS The invention of the automobile caused a revolution in transportation. Each year after 1900 the automobile became better and more people found that they could afford to own one. This led to a demand for better roads. Nothing had been done about the roads of New York State since the days of the turnpikes. They were full of holes, filled with snow in the winter, mud in the spring and dust in the summer. No one wanted to spend tax money to fix the roads and so things stayed in this dreadful condition until the automobile owners demanded better roads.

Gradually, things began to improve and by 1910 the state was in the road building business. To pay for the roads, which it built between the big cities, the state said that automobile owners had to buy automobile licenses. Later a tax was placed on each gallon of gasoline. Both of these methods are still followed today. In addition, all states now receive help from the federal government in their road building program.

THE THRUWAY The greatest achievement of the state in road building was the building of the New York State Thruway. This great highway, which was opened in 1955, is a modern turnpike because those who use it must pay a toll. The Thruway is 427 miles long and connects New York City with Buffalo. When you add the spurs of the Thruway which connect it with Pennsylvania, New Jersey and Massachusetts, the road is 564 miles long. Many of you have ridden on the Thruway and know what a wonderful highway it is.

171

MORE EXPRESSWAYS In addition to the Thruway the state has built many other beautiful parkways and limited access highways. This means that you can enter and leave these highways only at certain places. There is no toll on these highways. Some examples are the Northway which goes from Albany to Canada and the highway from Binghamton and Elmira to Syracuse. Still others are being planned for the future.

Courtesy of the New York State Department of Commerce

A modern tunnel

BRIDGES AND TUNNELS An exciting part of the state's building program has been the building of bridges and tunnels. Some of these have made it easier to get into New York City. The beautiful suspension bridge across the Hudson, named after George Washington, is an example of these bridges. It is one of the longest suspension bridges in the world. The Holland Tunnel, which was built by the states of New Jersey and New York together, goes under the Hudson River and connects the two states. It is used by millions of people every day. The Lincoln Tunnel has three tubes. One goes from Manhattan to New Jersey. One goes to Long Island City and the third goes to Brooklyn. The building of the tunnels was exciting and full of danger. Perhaps you would like to read more about it in other books your librarian can suggest.

Other bridges have been built by the state across the Hudson, Mohawk, Niagara and St. Lawrence Rivers.

THE PORT OF AUTHORITY AND THE THRUWAY AUTHORITY

To operate the Thruway and the Port of New York the state legislature created two groups. One is the Port of New York Authority. The other is the Thruway Authority. Each of these groups is responsible for seeing that its activity is well-managed for the good of the state. They set up the rules and regulations which must be followed by the people who use the port and the thruway.

THE AIRPLANE

During the last twenty-five years something new has been added to the state's transportation story. That something is the airplane. Since 1925 air transportation has become increasingly important to all of us. Thousands of people now travel by air. New York City, of course, became a terminal for all the leading airlines. LaGuardia Airport was built in 1939 but was soon found to be too small. In 1948 Idlewild Airport*on Jamaica Bay was opened. So many people use these two airports that they are always being improved and expanded. Most of us think of airplanes as carrying only people, but the amount of air freight and air express increases every year. Almost everything is shipped by air — heavy machinery — racehorses — lobsters. Goods that are delicate and easily spoiled, such as flowers and fruit, are often sent by air because it is faster. The amount of air mail also grows each year. The airplane has truly become a most important part of the transportation story.

* Renamed Kennedy International Airport in 1964.

173

To Help You Remember . . .

1. Why is it possible for a few farmers to supply New York with the agricultural products it needs?
2. Where was the first agricultural college located? When was it started?
3. Why do we have agricultural experiment stations?
4. What is New York's chief agricultural product?
5. What changes have taken place in the location of industries?
6. What problems do unions try to solve?
7. What is meant by "workmen's compensation"?
8. What is the meaning of "unemployment insurance"?
9. Name three important railroads in New York after the Civil War. Tell which part of the state each railroad served.
10. Give a reason for the decline of railroad transportation.
11. Give an important result of the invention of the automobile.

The Wonderful World of Words . . .

1. authority
2. tunnel
3. access
4. limited access
5. spurs
6. depression
7. insurance
8. compensation
9. craft

Perhaps You Would Like to . . .

1. Make a report to the class on one of the following topics:
   1. The Brooklyn Bridge
   2. The George Washington Bridge
   3. The Building of the Holland Tunnel
2. Write a report on the life of Cornelius Vanderbilt and the New York Central Railroad.
3. Write a report on the problems facing the railroads today.
4. Write an article for the newspaper asking for better working conditions in the factories. Use the Triangle Fire as an example.
5. Pretend that you are an immigrant working in a factory in New York City in 1910. Write a letter back to your relatives explaining why you joined a union.

174

Chapter XIII

RECENT SOCIAL AND CULTURAL DEVELOPMENTS IN NEW YORK STATE

CHAPTER XIII

1. Changes in Population

Let us think now for awhile about some of the other things which have happened to New York since 1865, when the Civil War ended. To begin, let's think about the **people** of New York State.

POPULATION TRENDS In 1860 there were almost four million people in New York State. Many of these people were immigrants, who had come to seek a new life in the New World. As we know, the Irish and the Germans came to work on the canal and the railroads. During the Civil War not many immigrants came to America. As soon as the war was over, America again threw open her doors and the people from Europe came pouring in. For the most part, the immigrants came from northern Europe — Germany, Sweden, Norway, Denmark, England, and France. The greatest numbers still came from Germany and Ireland. Most of the Irish stayed in New York City, but many Germans went to upstate cities to find homes.

All of this changed around 1900. People still came in large numbers, but they were a different kind of people. Now, the immigrants to America came from southern and eastern Europe. They came from Poland, Italy, Russia, Greece, and Hungary. They, too, were poor. There was no hope for them in their own countries. There, they would always be poor and without land of their own. In America, the land of opportunity, there was hope that a man could have plenty to eat if he would work hard. He might even get rich! And so they came to work in the mills and mines, to sew in the factories, to farm the land, to enrich America. Sometimes whole families came together. Often only one would come at first. He would work hard for a few years, save his money, and then send for the rest of the family.

QUOTAS ARE SET   When World War I came in 1917, very few immigrants could come to America. Laws were passed by Congress setting limits on the number of immigrants who could come into the country. However, when World War II was over, several hundred thousand persons were allowed to enter America as immigrants because they had suffered so much under the German and Russian rule.

As each group of foreigners came to America most of them settled down where they could see familiar faces, hear a familiar language, and live the way they were used to living. This meant that most of the foreigners who stayed in New York State settled in New York City or one of the other large cities. Because they liked to live together, Little Italys, Chinatowns, and other nationality groups grew up. However, this did not mean that the new immigrants did not become good American citizens. Schools and settlement houses held classes just for immigrants. Here they were taught the English language and how to became citizens of our country.

Each group of newcomers has made our state and nation richer, more interesting places in which to live. They have brought with them skills, abilities, and arts which America needed.

Immigrants from foreign lands are not the only people who have moved into New York State and helped to make it great. Many people from our own states have left their homes and come to New York to live. Young people come from every state in the Union. They hope to make their fortune in the biggest city in the country.

Negroes have always lived in New York State. However, it was during World War I that Negroes began to leave the South and come to New York by the thousands. The war factories needed workers. The Negroes wanted to leave their poor life in the South. They came to New York and settled in a part of Manhattan called Harlem. Life is both good and bad in Harlem.

177

There are fine homes and beautiful apartment houses for rich Negroes. The poor Negroes often have to live in very ugly, very crowded, very dirty places. These places are called slums. The rent is often high in the slums. There are churches and schools in Harlem. Harlem even has its own newspaper, the **Amsterdam News.** Many famous people grew up in Harlem. You have all heard of Willie Mays, haven't you? Althea Gibson, the famous tennis star, also grew up on Harlem streets. Negroes have given us leaders in many fields. Perhaps the most famous Negro today is Dr. Ralph Bunche who holds a high office in the United Nations.

The newest newcomers to New York are the people from Puerto Rico. These people are citizens of the United States so there is no limit on how many can come into the country each year. Thousands of them come. They, too, live close together. Their part of New York City is called Spanish Harlem because everyone there speaks Spanish. Most of the Puerto Ricans are very poor and have not had much training. For the most part they work at trades which take very little skill.

In 1960, the last time that population was counted, New York State had over 16 million people. This was more than any other state in the nation except California. There are three main reasons for New York's large population.

(1) More children are born each year.

(2) Fewer people die now than in earlier years.

(3) People come to New York from Europe, Puerto Rico and other parts of the United States.

We have read earlier that today most New Yorkers live in cities instead of on farms. Most New Yorkers also live in a narrow strip which stretches across the state, then turns and follows the Hudson River to the ocean. This is called the "Population Belt." It contains the largest cities of New York State. Almost half of the people in the state live in New York City. Since 1930 many people have left the cities to live in the "suburbs." This means small towns which lie just at the edge of the cities. New York State is rich in many things. This includes her great population.

2. New York Is the Nation's Fine Arts Center

Every country has a culture of its own. When we use the word culture in this way we mean art, science, literature, theater and music. For many years New York City has been the center of the cultural life of the United States. Every artist or actor or writer or musician hopes that some day he can work in New York. Most of the books and magazines are published in New York. Most of the important artists live and work in New York. The radio and television studios in New York are the biggest and most important. In New York there are schools where young people can be trained in the arts of writing, acting, singing, dancing, etc. There are also great universities and libraries in the city.

Courtesy of the New York State Department of Commerce
New York Public Library

179

THE THEATERS If you want to be an actor or actress, then surely you will want to go to New York City some day. Broadway is the area where the country's great playhouses are located. This has been true ever since the Shubert brothers opened their first theater more than sixty years ago. When the movies came along, the theater business was hurt because people wanted to see the new pictures instead of live actors. However, in recent years, the theater has come back and now the playhouses are crowded. Some plays go on for three or four years. It is often hard to get a ticket. In addition to the Broadway plays, there are now good plays being given "off-Broadway." These plays often have very good young actors in them. They cost less than the Broadway plays. To work in New York is the dream of every actor.

MUSIC New York City is also the leader in music in our country. One of the reasons for this is that there are enough people in New York City to support fine music

Courtesy of the New York State Department of Commerce
Philharmonic Hall

concerts of all kinds as well as opera and musical plays. Another reason is that the famous players and singers from Europe always come to New York City first. The Metropolitan Opera Company is one of the world's greatest opera companies. The New York Philharmonic is one of the world's greatest symphony orchestras. Soon both of these groups will be located in the beautiful new Lincoln Center for the Performing Arts. This new building will really make New York City the capital of the music world! Other cities in New York also have fine music. The most important is Rochester where the famous Eastman School of Music is located. Almost every other city in New York State has a symphony orchestra.

Perhaps you like popular music better than classical? New York City leads there, too. In fact, most of the popular music written today is published and recorded in New York City. This is where Tin Pan Alley is located. Now, of course, that isn't a real alley. It's not even one certain street. It is just a name given to the popular music business. This business gives you all the songs you hear on juke-boxes and television and Broadway shows. Some outstanding writers of popular songs have been Irving Berlin and Richard Rodgers. George Gershwin wrote not only popular songs; he also wrote **Porgy and Bess,** the most famous American opera.

THE MUSEUMS   New York City is a city of museums. Some of the most wonderful art of all the world has been collected and placed in the museums of New York City for you to see. The greatest of all of these museums is, of course, the Metropolitan Museum of Art. Here you can see great paintings and great sculpture from all over the wold. You can even go inside a real Egyptian tomb! Millions of people visit this museum each year to share the wonderful things it owns. In fact, over three million people visited it in 1960! Other famous museums in New York City are the Museum of Modern Art, the Whitney Museum of American Art and the new Guggenheim Museum. There are good art museums in cities all over New York State. Perhaps you have been to the Rochester Museum or to the Albany Institute of History and

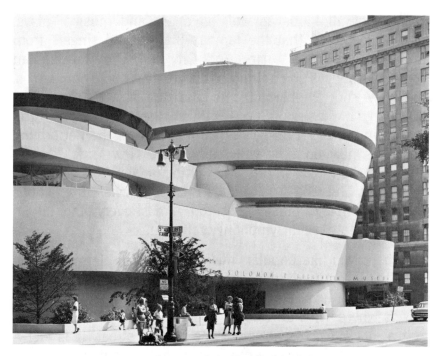

Guggenheim Museum

Art. The folk-art at Fenimore House in Cooperstown is an exciting collection to see.

LITERATURE Literature is also part of the culture. In the years after the Civil War, New York City also became the leader in this field. Most of the books and magazines were published in New York. The country's greatest newspapers, such as The New York Times and The New York Herald-Tribune, grew up in New York. Many of the country's best writers came to live and work in New York.

Some of the New York writers you should remember are: John Burroughs, Edward Wescott, Samuel Hopkins Adams, Walter Edmonds and Carl Carmer. Burroughs wrote about nature and the joys and excitement of outdoor life. Wescott wrote the book called **David Harum.** Samuel Hopkins Adams wrote about life in early New York and the Erie Canal. You will certainly enjoy his **Grandfather Stories** and his **Erie Canal.** Carl

182

Carmer still writes about New York State history and folklore. Read his **Rebellion at Quaker Hill** or **Windfall Fiddle**. Walter Edmunds wrote the exciting **Drums Along the Mohawk.**

**NEW YORK CITY
A CULTURAL LEADER**
New York City is the leader of the cultural life of our state and nation. This does not mean, however, that you find culture **only** in New York City. People all over the state are interested in art, music, writing, and acting. Nearly every city has a museum and its artists show their pictures to the public in small art shows. In fact, more and more people have begun to paint since World War II. Every city has a little-theater group which gives several plays each year. In almost every community there are handicraft groups which meet at the Y. W. C. A. or in homes for the purpose of making lovely things. People who like to sing can always find a choral group to join and those who play instruments can almost always find a group with which to play. Not only New York City, but all of New York State, as well, leads a full and rich cultural life.

THE CAPITAL CITY OF THE WORLD
New York City can also be called the capital city of the world. The reason for this is that the United Nations has its headquarters here. In 1946 the Rockefeller family gave a large piece of land, about seventeen acres, along the East River to the United Nations. Here the beautiful headquarters buildings were built. You have all seen pictures of the glass-walled Secretariat building. Did you know that its marble sides came from Vermont? In this building the employees of the United Nations work, typing, mimeographing, translating. In the lower assembly building delegates from all over the world, representing one hundred and eleven nations, meet to talk over the problems of the world. This is the most important building in New York City and the reason why we can call New York the world capital.

To Help You Remember . . .
1. Where did most of New York's immigrants come from between the Civil War and 1900?
2. Where did most of the immigrants come from after 1900?

3. Where did most of the immigrants settle? Why?
4. Who are the newest newcomers to New York State? Where do they live?
5. Give the three reasons for New York's large population.
6. Where do most of the people of New York State live?
7. Give four examples to prove that New York City is the cultural center of our nation.
8. Name four modern writers who come from New York. Tell what each has written.
9. Why can New York City be called the "capital of the world"?

The Wonderful World of Words ...

1. culture
2. choral
3. symphony
4. suburbs

Perhaps You Would Like to ...

1. Look up more material on one of the people mentioned in this chapter and make a report to the class on that person.
2. Look up more facts about the new Lincoln Center for the Performing Arts and make a report. The Readers' Guide will help you find the material you need.
3. Read parts of the book "Only in America" by Harry Golden to learn of Jewish life in New York City in the early days of this century.
4. Find out all you can about the problems of the Puerto Ricans in our country. The Readers' Guide will help.
5. Make a series of posters which show how people from other lands have made New York a more interesting state.
6. Make a collection of postcards or pictures of the famous museums, libraries and universities in our state. Put these together to form a display.
7. Make a bulletin board display using the book jackets of books written by New York authors. Your librarian can help you with this project.

Chapter XIV

SOME OUTSTANDING
NEW YORK GOVERNORS

1. Samuel J. Tilden
2. Grover Cleveland
3. Theodore Roosevelt
4. Charles Evans Hughes
5. Alfred E. Smith
6. Franklin Delano Roosevelt
7. Herbert H. Lehman
8. Thomas E. Dewey

CHAPTER XIV

SOME OUTSTANDING NEW YORK GOVERNORS

New York has had many fine governors during its long history. These men have helped New York grow as a democracy. Let us read about some of these men and see how each of them helped to bring good government to the Empire State.

Samuel J. Tilden

1. Samuel J. Tilden

The first governor we shall read about is Samuel Tilden. Tilden was born in Columbia County in 1814 and grew up to be one of the richest and best-known lawyers in the United States in the years just after the Civil War. He was also interested in politics. He believed always in good, clean, honest government. Because of this the Democratic Party asked him to run for governor of the State in 1874. The people elected him to this office by a big majority.

While he was governor, Tilden saw to it that laws were passed which made it very hard for men in government to be dishonest. Samuel Tilden is best remembered for breaking up the famous "Canal Ring." The Legislature had said that the Erie Canal must be repaired and made larger. The "Canal Ring" was a group of men in government who "made a deal" with the contractors who worked on the Canal. The contractors charged the State far too much for the work they did. Then the dishonest contractors and politicians divided the extra money. Governor Tilden got evidence to prove that this was going on. Then he went to the Legislature and told the whole thing. The Canal

Ring was smashed! This saved the taxpayers of New York millions of dollars.

The Democratic Party was so pleased with Tilden's record as governor that they asked him to run for President in 1876. The Republican candidate was Rutherford B. Hayes. It was a very close race. When the election was over no one was sure who had won. A special committee was set up by Congress to go over all the election results and decide the winner. This committee finally decided that Rutherford B. Hayes had won the election.

Though Samuel J. Tilden failed to become President of the United States, he did serve the people of New York faithfully and well as one of its finest governors.

Grover Cleveland

2. Grover Cleveland

Grover Cleveland was born in New Jersey in 1837. When he was very young the family moved to New York State. First the Clevelands lived in Fayetteville and then in Clinton. When the father died in 1852, the son realized that he could not go to Hamilton College as he had planned. He knew that he would have to educate himself in some way. He took all the money he had — twenty-five dollars — and went west to Buffalo. There he found a place to work in a law office. Four years later he had learned enough law so that he could become a lawyer and have his own law office.

Cleveland's first public office came in 1863 when he was asked to be the Assistant District Attorney for Erie County.

187

Buffalo is the big city in Erie County. In 1869 Cleveland was elected Sheriff of Erie County. After one term as sheriff he settled down to being a lawyer. He became one of the best-known lawyers in western New York. In 1881 the people of Buffalo elected Grover Cleveland as their mayor.

In 1882 the Democratic Party nominated Cleveland for governor of the state. He won the election easily. While he was governor a good civil service law was passed. Civil service is another way of saying government service. This law was about all the jobs the Government needed to have done. Governor Cleveland believed strongly that only good, able men should be in government. He is the man who said, "A public office is a public trust." He would appoint only the best men to government jobs. He often did not pay much attention to what the Democratic Party leaders wanted.

In 1884 the Democrats nominated Grover Cleveland to run for President. He won the election. He was the fourth New Yorker to become President of the United States.

Theodore Roosevelt

3. Theodore Roosevelt

Theodore Roosevelt was born in New York City in 1858. As a boy he spent much of his time at his father's country house at Oyster Bay on Long Island. Here, by rowing and swimming in Long Island Sound, and by tramping through the woods, he made his weak body into a strong one. He also took boxing lessons in order to make his body stronger. He loved Oyster Bay and made it his home when he was older.

Theodore Roosevelt decided early in his life that he wanted to be in politics, he wanted to have something to do with government. He did not wait long to begin. The year after he finished Harvard College he was elected to the State Assembly of New York. This was in 1881. He was elected again in 1882 and again in 1883. In fact, in 1883 when he was only twenty-four years old, the Republicans suggested that he be made Speaker of the Assembly!

In 1884, Roosevelt decided to go out West to live for awhile. He bought two ranches on the Little Missouri River in North Dakota. Here he lived the life of a cowboy for two years. After that he was always interested in the problems of the west, particularly problems of conservation.

After he returned from the West, Roosevelt served as President of the Board of Police Commissioners for the City of New York. For two hard, action-packed years he fought criminals and racketeers, and dishonest people in the City Government. He left this job to become Assistant Secretary of the Navy in Washington.

When the Spanish-American War broke out, Theodore Roosevelt could not stay at home. He organized some of his cowboy and college friends into the famous Rough Riders and went off to war. The Rough Riders fought bravely and well, especially at the Battle of San Juan Hill.

After the war was over, Theodore Roosevelt returned to New York State. The Republican Party asked him to run for governor. He did and was elected by a large number of votes.

While Roosevelt was Governor of New York, many good laws were passed. Some of the laws made the State Government more honest. Many more State jobs were put under the merit system. This means that only people who could really do the jobs were given jobs in the State Government. Some of the best laws were those which tried to help the working people. Laws were passed to help make working safer for women and children in the factories of the State. More factory inspectors were required to see that the laws were obeyed by the factory owners. Working conditions were improved for the workers in many industries. Governor Roosevelt even tried to do away with the terrible piece-work system which employed many women in their homes for low wages. Another thing which started while Theodore Roosevelt was governor was the effort to get better, cleaner and safer houses for the poor people in the cities. Theodore Roosevelt was governor for only two years. Then he was nominated for vice-president of the United States when William McKinley was running for President. McKinley and Roosevelt won. Not long after, someone killed President McKinley and so Theodore Roosevelt took his place as President. He was the fifth New Yorker to serve as President of the United States.

4. Charles Evans Hughes

Charles Evans Hughes was one of the leading governors of New York State. He did not intend to have a career in politics as Roosevelt did. Hughes was a lawyer in New York City. No one knew very much about him until he led investigations of the

Charles Evans Hughes

gas and insurance companies in New York City. He discovered that both kinds of companies had been cheating the people in a terrible way. The investigations made Hughes famous and the Republican Party nominated him for governor. He won the election easily.

190

Charles Evans Hughes served two terms as governor of New York. During those two terms many laws were passed which made our government more honest and more democratic. A public service commission was started. The purpose of this commission was to see that such companies as gas and electric companies and transportation companies (streetcars, buses and railroads) were run for the good of the people who needed them.

Hughes was in favor of many new ideas for making our democratic government work better. He also was a friend of the working man. While he was governor he signed fifty-six laws which helped and protected the workers of New York State.

Charles Evans Hughes resigned as governor in 1910 to become a justice of the United States Supreme Court.

Alfred E. Smith

One of the most popular governors New York State ever had was a man named Alfred E. Smith. He was also one of the greatest men our state has ever had. Al Smith was a New York City boy, born in the slums, and forced to work hard from the time he was a little boy.

When he was still a very young man Smith joined the Democratic Party. He rose quickly in the opinion of the party leaders because he was quick and eager to learn, he had a very pleasant personality and he was intelligent. In 1903 this young man who had been born in a slum, was elected to the State Assembly. And the people in his New York neighborhood kept on electing him year after year. When Smith had been an assemblyman for ten years, he was elected Speaker of the Assembly. This means that he was the leader of the Assembly.

In 1918 Alfred E. Smith was elected governor of New York for the first time. He served two years. He served as governor again from 1922 to 1928. During his years as governor he fought hard for better government in New York State. Because of Governor Smith our state government runs more smoothly. He was able to see what really needed to be done and to find the right way of getting things done. He knew that the governor needed help in running the state government. He set up the eighteen departments which now make up the executive branch of our government.

Alfred E. Smith

While Alfred E. Smith was governor many very fine laws were passed, laws which helped many people. To help the working man, a forty-eight-hour week was made legal. Also, workers who were hurt while on the job received more money than they had in the past. Schools were helped, too. The State gave more money for education and teachers' salaries were raised. For the first time women teachers received the same pay as men teachers. Conditions inside the State's prisons were improved. The hospitals for the insane were increased and made better. Governor Smith didn't forget his home town either. A law was passed which gave New York City more power to govern itself.

Al Smith was a great governor. He was deeply respected by the people of the State. Because of his warm and colorful personality the people also loved him. In 1928 he ran for the Presidency but was defeated by Herbert Hoover. He was never in politics after that.

Franklin Delano Roosevelt

6. Franklin Delano Roosevelt

When Al Smith decided to run for the Presidency in 1928 he asked a man named Roosevelt to run for governor of New York. Who was this man? His name was Franklin Delano Roosevelt and he was from the same family as Theodore Roosevelt. The two men were distant cousins. He was trained as a lawyer, but liked government service better. He had been a member of the State Senate. He had also been Assistant Secretary of the Navy. He had run for Vice-President of the United States but had been defeated. He was crippled. Polio had struck him and left him badly crippled legs. For many years he wore heavy braces in order to stand. He won the election in 1928 and set out upon a long career of service to his State and Nation.

In many ways Franklin D. Roosevelt carried on the kind of government which Al Smith had started. Both men had the same ideas about honesty in government, helping the poor, and better working conditions for the laboring man. Roosevelt also agreed with Smith that the State should have its own electric power industry to make sure that the people were treated honestly and fairly.

Soon after Franklin Roosevelt became governor the Depression came. This was a time when millions of men were out of work. There were few jobs and very little money for anyone. People who had been rich were suddenly very poor. Something had to be done. If the people could not help themselves, someone else must help them. Governor Roosevelt saw that the

193

state came to the aid of the poor people. The State created jobs for those who had no work. Old people were given money to live on. Governor Roosevelt earned the admiration of many people for the way he governed New York State during those terrible days.

In 1932 Franklin Roosevelt ran for the Presidency of the United States. He was elected by a great majority. He served as President of the United States for twelve years, longer than any other man had ever served. He was the sixth New Yorker to be President of the United States.

Herbert H. Lehman

7. Herbert H. Lehman

When Franklin Roosevelt left Albany and moved to Washington, he had to resign as governor of New York State. This meant that the lieutenant-governor became governor until the next election. The new governor's name was Herbert H. Lehman. He became one of the greatest governors New York has ever had. The people respected him so much that they elected him governor three times.

Herbert Lehman carried on the good work of Smith and Roosevelt and added a great deal of his own. He did not believe in expensive government; he believed that money **should** be saved. He also believed that a state government could save money. To prove this, while he was governor he paid off the great debt which the State owed when he became governor.

While he was governor, Herbert Lehman saw to it that low-rent housing projects were built for people who needed a decent place to live. Laws were passed which helped many people such as laborers in factories, school teachers and dairy farmers.

8. Thomas E. Dewey

Thomas E. Dewey was born in Michigan. However, he went to law school at Columbia University and after that he decided to become a New Yorker. He first became famous when Governor Lehman appointed him a special prosecutor and told him to investigate racketeering in New York City. Do you know

Thomas E. Dewey

what a racketeer is? He is a gangster or criminal who threatens innocent people unless they give him money regularly. For instance, a racketeer might tell a grocery store owner that his store would be bombed unless the grocer turned over part of his profit each week to the gangster. There were many of these gangsters in New York City during the 1930's. It was Dewey's job to find them, get evidence on them and put them in jail. He succeeded very well. He did such a good job that he was elected District Attorney of New York City. After that, even more gangsters left the Country or went to jail.

In 1938 the Republicans asked Dewey to run for governor. He did but did not win. He tried again in 1942 and won. He remained governor of New York State for twelve years.

195

World War II was going on when Dewey first became governor. He saw that New York played its full part in the war effort. Many war industries were located in New York State. Governor Dewey saw that things went smoothly in those industries. He set up a labor board which would settle quarrels between the workers and the owners. He set up places where mothers could leave their children while they went to work in the war plants.

After the war was over, Governor Dewey began to look at other problems in the State. One was the problem of discrimination because of religion, or color. The Quinn-Ives Act, passed in 1945, makes it against the law to refuse any person a job because of his religion or color. The Act set up a board of five men to see that the law is obeyed. This law is one of which New Yorkers can be proud. It is a real step forward in democracy.

Another problem which the State had after the war was in the field of transportation. Good roads were needed badly. None had been built during the war. The answer was the building of the Thruway and the planning of several other main highways. The Thruway, as you know, makes it possible to go all the way from Yonkers to Buffalo without a single crossroad or traffic light.

While Dewey was still governor the State created the State University. Education was given more money and the State began to spend money on medical research. All of this tells you that the state government has become more and more concerned about the lives of its citizens.

APPENDIX

This book ends with Chapter XIII on page 184. Events have been brought up to date as of June, 1965.

Chapter XIV—SOME OUTSTANDING GOVERNORS—has been added as an enrichment section. Most of our governors have rendered outstanding service to the state and nation. However, events occurred in these eight governors' administrations which enabled them to demonstrate their capabilities and to permit them to become national figures. These events should be common knowledge to all social studies students.

INDEX